Idiots in Love

Other Books by Leland Gregory

What's the Number for 911?
What's the Number for 911 Again?
The Stupid Crook Book
Hey, Idiot!
Idiots at Work
Bush-Whacked

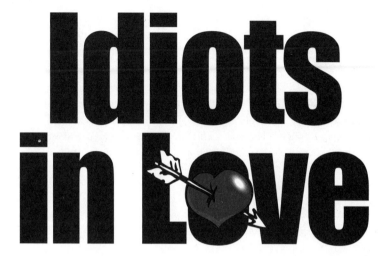

Idiots in Love

Chronicles of Romantic Stupidity

Leland Gregory

**Andrews McMeel
Publishing, LLC**

Kansas City

06 07 08 09 10 MLT 10 9 8 7 6 5 4 3 2 1

ISBN-13: 978-0-7407-5669-6
ISBN-10: 0-7407-5669-9

Library of Congress Control Number: 2005933690

Design by Holly Camerlinck

Attention: Schools and Businesses

Andrews McMeel books are available at quantity discounts with bulk purchase for educational, business, or sales promotional use. For information, please write to: Special Sales Department, Andrews McMeel Publishing, LLC, 4520 Main Street, Kansas City, Missouri 64111.

Two-for-One Deal

t was a wedding present that the future bride and groom would never forget. During their engagement party in Tirana, Albania, the teenage lovebirds were surprised by more than just a toaster; the groom's father and the bride's mother fell in love and eloped. During their honeymoon in Greece, the future in-laws became wanted outlaws when each called their respective spouse asking for a divorce. The teenagers, who finally did get married, are concerned because if the couple has a child, the new groom could eventually wind up becoming his own grandfather. ♥

STUDY FINDS SEX, PREGNANCY LINK

—*Cornell Daily Sun*, December 7, 1995

Things That Go Bump in the Night

A middle-aged woman in England was awakened by a strange noise in her house and immediately called the police. The bobbies arrived promptly and scoured the residence looking for the source of the sound. The woman's face went from "white with fear" to "red with embarrassment" when the police discovered an intruder of another sort had caused the noise; the woman's sex toy had gone off in her nightstand. A spokesperson for the police said the officers on call had a difficult time keeping straight faces when they apprehended the apparatus. I suppose the term "assault and battery" would apply here—for her next assault she'll need new batteries. ♥

In Detroit, Michigan, it is unlawful to use any kind of pennant to decorate your car in order to be noticed or to impress your girlfriend.

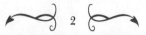

A Clique Come True

n January 1996, Stewart Marshall was found guilty of assaulting his wife. After announcing the verdict, Judge Joel Gehrke called Marshall to the bench and ordered him to hold out his hand. Marshall did as he was told, and Judge Gehrke gave him a light three-fingered slap on the wrist and admonished him by saying, "Don't do that!" This action started a whirlwind of public outrage against the judge, but Gehrke felt the simple punishment was justified, since Marshall's wife had become pregnant by Marshall's brother and had recently given birth to Marshall's nephew. ♥

The ancient Egyptians used **crocodile dung** as a contraceptive.
[Author's note: I can see how that would work, can't you?]
But it was the use of the acacia plant that yielded the best results.
Even today, the active ingredients in the acacia plant
are found in spermicidal jellies and creams.

—*The History of Sex,* the History Channel, August 1999

Keeping the
Fizz in the Marriage

Amanda Blake of Northampton, Massachusetts, who had been a loyal employee of the Coca-Cola Bottling Company for eight years, was discovered to be a traitor. Coca-Cola found out that Blake had fallen in love with and become engaged to David Cronin, who worked for archrival Pepsi. Coke demanded that Blake either break off her engagement, persuade Cronin to leave Pepsi, or resign from her position at Coca-Cola. Blake nearly popped her top when she was given these options and decided not to do anything of the sort. Coca-Cola promptly fired her for "conflict of interest." But Blake spun the bottle on Coca-Cola and sued for damages, winning a $600,000 settlement. Now that's the real thing! ♥

Don't Pass This Way Again!

he South Dakota Supreme Court upheld a ruling in September 1994, citing the husband as the cause of a couple's troubles. The husband had, among other bad habits, a tendency to pass gas around the house and get angry with his wife when she complained. The wife claimed her husband could easily regulate his odiferous emissions and would break wind as a "retaliation thing." ♥

In Michigan:

"Cohabitation by divorced parties:
If any persons after being divorced
from the bonds of matrimony for any
cause whatever, shall cohabit
together, they shall be liable to
all the penalties provided by law
against adultery."

—750.32, Michigan Penal Code Act 328 of 1931

Wedding Blitz

ollywood celebrities are known for having short marriages—just think of Britney Spears's fifty-five-hour union. But even that couldn't top one of the shortest marriages on record—ninety minutes. In June 2003, after a whirlwind eight-week romance, Scott McKie and Victoria Anderson tied the knot, and then Scott tied one on. During their reception at an upscale pub, Scott started to behave "disgracefully" and was "drinking like a Russian fish." McKie scrambled on top of a table and gave a toasted "toast" to his wife's bridesmaids and made suggestive comments to some of the female guests. To show her appreciation, Vicky christened her new husband over the head with an ashtray. When the bartender cut him off, Scott grabbed a hat stand and threw it javelin style at a large mirror. The number of wedding guests increased when the police arrived, and Scott greeted them, not with a handshake, but with a head butt. While Scott was being dragged down the aisle to jail, Vicky canceled their honeymoon reservations and started the divorce proceedings. Total marriage time: ninety minutes. Memories that will last a lifetime: priceless. ♥

Did Ya Hear the One About…?

After most weddings someone, usually the groom's friends, plays a prank on the newly married couple. After being married only a month, Raul Hortena realized the joke was on him when he appeared in front of a Barcelona court asking for a divorce. The judge turned down the request because he discovered that Raul-the-Fool had used invisible ink when he signed his marriage certificate. The *Guardian* reported that Raul was also fined approximately $200 for forging an official document. ♥

BONNIE BLOWS CLINTON

Article concerning Hurricane Bonnie hitting Clinton, North Carolina.
—*Sampson Independent,* August 27, 1998

Matching Ring and Bracelet

aymond Rashawne Carter proposed to his girlfriend in February 2005 and then surprised her with a beautiful set of wedding rings worth $1,500. She accepted his proposal, and he slipped the engagement ring on her finger, but it was a little big. The unfazed fiancé decided to return the rings and have them resized. At the Charlottesville, Virginia, store, the clerk took the rings and then gave the police a ring. Apparently, Raymond forgot to mention that he didn't pay for the jewelry. So in procuring the rings at a five-finger discount in order to adorn his girlfriend's ring finger, Raymond fingered himself, and I'm sure his girlfriend gave him the finger for his efforts. ♥

When Ruth and Kevin Kimber married in 1990, she was ninety-three and he was twenty-eight.

Monkey Business

D arwin was right—we are descended from monkeys. . . . Well, at least men are. A study conducted by Duke University, in January 2005, showed that male monkeys would give up their juice rewards in order to look at pictures of female monkeys' bottoms. Since monkeys don't have money, choosing pictures over juice is akin to paying for the images, and they don't have Internet access, either. The rhesus macaque monkeys also splurged on photos of higher-ranking primates but had to be bribed with juice to make them look at lower-ranking monkeys. It has been rumored that *Hustler* founder, Larry Flynt, is considering publishing *Porn-orangutan* with a "Pri-mate" centerfold of the month. ♥

Sign in a Zurich hotel:

BECAUSE OF THE IMPROPRIETY OF ENTERTAINING GUESTS OF THE OPPOSITE SEX IN THE BEDROOM, IT IS SUGGESTED THAT THE LOBBY BE USED FOR THIS PURPOSE.

Is That a Nightstick in Your Pocket or Are You Just Happy to See Me?

In June 2003, Officer Jamie Hope was dispatched to a residence after receiving several noise complaints. When he knocked on the door at the bachelorette party in Gainesville, Florida, the partygoers assumed he was the hired entertainment. While the officer was speaking to guest of honor Nichole Neal, the other guests yelled, "The warning has gone far enough—when are you going to start stripping?" It took them a while to realize that handcuffing Neal wasn't part of his kinky act. He was actually arresting her on an outstanding warrant. Not wanting to have their party ruined, the guests followed the patrol car to the station and paid Neal's bail so they could return to the festivities. ♥

Fifty-eight percent of women cuddle after sex, but eight percent just "lie there silently."

Ring in the Holidays

Being the very model of a modern mature woman, Janne Grim decided she would propose to her boyfriend as opposed to the traditional vice versa. The young Norwegian woman invited her boyfriend, Svein Froeytland, to a Christmas party and hid the wedding ring in his porridge. She watched impatiently as he wolfed down the porridge, but when he didn't mention the ring she took that as a no. After swallowing her pride, Janne told Svein about the proposed proposal, and he told her he must have swallowed the ring. He accepted her proposal and, borrowing a ring from one of the guests, made the engagement official. Svein said, "Now that I am twenty-four carats heavier, I will have to wait for nature to take its course. Then the ring will take its course, and everything will work out in the end." ♥

CHICK ACCUSES SOME OF HER MALE COLLEAGUES OF SEXISM

Article concerning allegations of sexism from
then-councilwoman, now Los Angeles city controller, Laura Chick.
—*Los Angeles Times,* June 23, 1998

May I Have the Envelope, Please!

survey taken in Britain, France, and Germany in February 2002 found that one in nine people admits to sending themselves Valentine's Day cards so they will get at least one. Of the remaining eight, one out of every three receives a card from their own children, and one in ten steals them from someone else in the house. ♥

A woman in Madrid, Spain, was shocked to discover that after five years of marriage, whenever her husband told her he was on a business trip he was actually taking **mass**. When she filed for divorce, Sandra Vega Martínez discovered that her husband, Jorge Barange, wasn't a businessman as he had told her. He was, in fact, a **Catholic priest**.

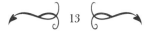

Captive Audience

Zambian court presided over by Judge Alfred Shilibwa granted a man a divorce on the grounds that his wife's suspicions and lack of commitment had permanently undermined their relationship. The judge was referring to the woman's habit of locking her husband in his bedroom every night so he wouldn't sneak out and have an affair. I can just imagine the man's cries for help: "Honey, I don't want to have an affair, I just want to go to the bathroom." ♥

A study of the effects of the abstinence-only **sex education** programs in Texas schools (spearheaded by then-governor George Bush) got a bad report. The study showed that 23 percent of ninth-grade girls had already had sex by the time they received the abstinence lessons, and after they attended, the percentage **increased**.

It Ain't Called a Jack-o'-Lantern for Nothing

n September 2002, a forty-five-year-old man in Warren, Michigan, was convicted of indecent exposure and sentenced to ninety days in jail. Police arrested the man after neighbors complained that he was naked in his backyard and was performing indecent acts with a pumpkin. When the man was approached by police he blurted out, "What, is it midnight already?" Sorry, I made up that last part. ♥

A JOB INTERVIEW IS NOT A DATE

—*New York Newsday*

Heating Things Up a Little

We've all heard the expression "Iron out your problems," but one eighteen-year-old bride from Andriasu, Romania, took this phrase too literally. After her husband, Mircea Stoleru, fell asleep without making love to her, she took matters into her own hands and burned him on the right shoulder with a hot iron. Stoleru took responsibility for his own inactions, and told reporters in July 2001, "This should serve me right. I knew what I got when I married such a young and beautiful wife, and I never get home sober." ♥

At their 1990 wedding in Seysinnet-Pariset, France, Fabien Pretou, standing **six feet two** inches tall, towered over his **three-feet-one-inch** bride Natalie Lucius.

♥ ♥ ♥

Longest marriage:
Wesley and Stella McGowen, married since February 6, 1920—more than 85 years.

—Guinness World Records 2005: Special 50th Anniversary Edition

Once, Twice, Three Times a Lady

A twenty-four-year-old woman in Beloit, Wisconsin, was charged with battery for allegedly hitting her husband with a plant stand, sending him to the hospital for six stitches. According to the police statement, the newlyweds frequently fought about sex. The night of the attack the woman became enraged because her husband decided to call it quits after only four sexual encounters with her that day. ♥

"[The victim] also has difficulty sleeping, driving his manual car and has lost his **libido**," ruled an Australian judge, who also awarded **$432,000** to the fifty-four-year-old man who'd lost his sex drive after being attacked by a **pig**.

Popping the Clutch

wo lovebirds from Naples, Italy, were fooling around at a local lovers' lane in their subcompact car when the car was accidentally hit from behind. The couple claimed they "lost control" during the collision and are suing to recover the expenses of their unplanned pregnancy. I guess the airbags weren't the only thing that deployed. ♥

"I was trying to drive her back to shore."

—Excuse used by a Pittsburgh man who was apparently throwing rocks at his wife as she struggled not to drown in the Kanawha River.

A Kodak Moment

A couple passing a photo booth at Paramount's Kings Island couldn't help popping in and having their picture taken. Police reported that the man casually mentioned to his girlfriend that they could have oral sex in this photo booth, and she agreed. Things quickly developed from there—including a copy of the photographs prominently displayed on a monitor outside the booth. The couple needed more than red-eye reduction after they were arrested on charges of public indecency. ♥

A Michigan jury awarded $200,000 to a twenty-seven-year-old man who claimed a car accident transformed him into a homosexual.

Actual book title:

TEACH YOURSELF SEX, 1951

Pieces of You

Moscow man with an explosive temper discovered his wife was having an affair and decided to pull the pin on the situation. According to police officials, the man was attempting to attach a bomb to the door of where he believed his wife and her lover were staying, when it detonated. I wonder if the woman prophesied about her relationship by saying, "If my husband finds out about us, he'll explode." ♥

PLENTY OF SEX ADVISED FOR SUCCESSFUL PREGNANCY

—Reuters headline, February 6, 2002

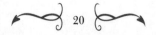

That's Difficult to Conceive

can't rule out the possibility of divine intervention by God," concluded a German judge after hearing the case of Birgit Weiss. Weiss claimed that God the Father was really God the father; that "He who formed the mountains" also formed a fetus. The woman claimed not to have had sex with anyone after she and her husband separated and genetic tests showed the child was not his. The estranged husband is accusing his former wife of attempting to defraud him of child support money. If her claim is true, I feel sorry for the next man she dates: "Oh, you're nothing like the last guy I was with." ♥

In October 2002, Mr. Rosaire Roy of Prince Albert, Saskatchewan, was sentenced to a year in jail for hiring someone to rob his store. Mr. Roy had arranged the robbery not to make money or collect insurance but to fulfill a **sexual fantasy**: He had the robber force him to undress along with a female acquaintance because he dreamed of being **tied up naked** with her.

♥ ♥ ♥

A soldier was dancing with a girl when she collapsed in his arms, after which he took her to his car and was intimate with her. He thought that she was drunk, but she was actually dead—*convicted:* attempted rape.

—*United States v. Thomas*, 31 C.M.A. 278; 32 C.M.R. 278 (1962)

Dude Looks Like a Lady

Here's an Extreme Makeover Gender Edition. Katherine is an Irish citizen living in Norfolk, Virginia, and she used to be a man named Damien. He/she is married to a guy named Pat, who used to be a woman named Patricia. With me so far? Okay, according to federal prosecutors, Katherine is in the country illegally and had a sex change to marry Pat, who had a sex change in order to hide from his/her former spouse, John Martin, whom he/she had never divorced. Since Pat is still legally married to another man, even though he's a man, too, his marriage to Katherine, who used to be a man, is not binding. Now the two have been indicted for defrauding the Immigration and Naturalization Service. I'm sure it will all boil down to a case of "he said/she said." ♥

A Streetcar Named Desire

The close quarters of a community theater, the long hours together, and the feeling of partnership provide the perfect breeding ground for a budding romance. But when fifty-three-year-old Jay Meisenhelder fell in love with a fellow thespian, things weren't all rosy—mainly because the girl was sixteen years old. Meisenhelder wrote the young actress an e-mail stating, ". . . Believe me, I know what love is. I love you as I have only loved two other women in my life." He persuaded the girl to meet him for a candlelit music session, where he served alcohol-free bananas Foster and played the sound track from *The Phantom of the Opera*. Strangely enough, she asked him to take her home. Meisenhelder, who is married (or was when this story broke) claimed, "Nothing I did was illegal." Which is technically true, since Indiana state law defines an adult as anyone sixteen years old or older. When his boss found out about the relationship, Meisenhelder was fired from his job as the Marion County, Indiana, Deputy Prosecutor and Assistant Chief of the Sex Crimes Division. This is the same Meisenhelder who made news in 2002 when he successfully prosecuted a photographer for child exploitation and possession of child pornography for taking nude pictures of seventeen-year-old girls. Meisenhelder insisted he was just "expressing a fantasy." ♥

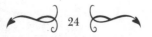

Boys Will Be Boys

The Department of Family and Children's Services had twenty-one-year-old Summer Jessica Strickland arrested immediately following the birth of her child. The Conyers, Georgia, woman was charged with statutory rape . . . of her husband, fourteen-year-old Tony Goss. Kissing-cousin jokes aside, the state of Georgia has no age limit on marriage as long as there is parental consent, so Strickland wasn't arrested because she married a minor—apparently that's okay. Prosecutors did argue that since Strickland and Goss conceived their child while Goss was only thirteen, and they were unmarried, she committed statutory rape. Does the state care that the two were legally married before the baby was born? Nope; their earlier sexual encounter was still illegal, prosecutors say, because Georgia law considers having sex with anyone under sixteen statutory rape—unless you're married to them. Which reminds me of the joke about the Georgia wife who says to her husband, "Honey, people say you're a pedophile." To which the husband responds, "That's an awfully big word for a thirteen-year-old." ♥

HUSBAND'S INTERNET DATE TURNS OUT TO BE HIS WIFE

—Ananova.com, July 19, 1994

Not-So-Sharp Shooter

A seventeen-year-old Pittsburgh girl was rushed to the hospital after her boyfriend went off half-cocked; actually, his gun went off half-cocked. The couple were involved in some bizarre bedroom activities when the .45-caliber handgun they were using as a prop fired and lodged a bullet in the girl's groin. The boyfriend was arrested and charged with aggravated assault, reckless endangerment, and corruption of a minor. ♥

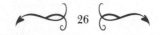

Stoned on the drug "ice," Tang Kwok-wai threw his eighteen-year-old girlfriend, Hong Kong waitress Ms. Au Wing-sze, over an eighteenth-floor balcony and stomped on her fingers as she clung to the rail. A downstairs neighbor saw the August 1999 incident and pulled Ms. Wing-sze to safety. Said Au's lawyer, "If anything, [the incident] has only strengthened [their] relationship." They plan to get married right after he is released from prison for his attempted-murder conviction.

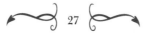

No-Fly Zone

In the January 2005 issue of *Current Biology*, researchers confirmed the truth of the age-old saying that "boys will be boys"—regardless of their species. It was discovered by a team from the University of Western Australia that for the opportunity to mate with a female, the male dance fly sometimes presented her with worthless tokens (cubic zirconium, in human terms). By the time the female discovers both the gift and the guy are worthless, however, the male dance fly has done the jitterbug and twirled away. ♥

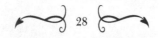

Pulling the Rug Out from Under Him

A man and his young bride invited a female friend over for drinks, and the phrase "Liquor is quicker" soon took on another meaning when the two women began making out. "Eye candy is dandy" but the Murfreesboro, Tennessee, man didn't want to be a passive observer, he wanted to be an active participant. Unfortunately, the man's wife didn't want him horning in on her girl's night out, so she kicked him out of the house. The man retaliated by calling the police. Apparently, while she was persuading her husband to leave the house, the woman allegedly scratched him, so he had her arrested and charged with domestic assault. It'll serve her right to be thrown in jail with hundreds of other lonely women—that'll show her! ♥

In West Virginia:

"It is a felony for a person at least fourteen to engage in sexual intercourse, sexual intrusion, or sexual contact with a person under twelve."

—West Virginia Code §§61-8B-3 (enacted 1976)

Keep on Truckin'

A Zambian man, Christopher Phiri, appeared in front of high court judges requesting a divorce from his wife, Naomi Kamanga, on grounds that she had an abortion and frequently came home late. Phiri was surprised when Judges Buxton Ng'andu and Robert Mwananshiku instead handed down a sentence of hard labor—in bed. The judges ordered Phiri to "stick to your wife and work harder in bed," reported Reuters. The judges told Phiri that he should keep his nose to the grindstone and get his wife pregnant, so they would be blessed with a baby, and their marriage would be saved. The court ordered Christopher and Naomi reconciled so they could obey the penal code. ♥

"This is so embarrassing. We had never done that before, and now she's in the hospital, and my cat's dead."

—In January 2005, after having made the decision to have sex, an unnamed New York City man and a female neighbor accidentally ignited a comforter with a candle and started a major fire in his apartment.

Mail and Female

Workers at a post office in Berlin, Germany, got quite a scare when one of the packages they were going to deliver started vibrating and made strange noises. Police questioned the man who had mailed the suspicious package, and he claimed it wasn't a bomb, but in order to work, it did have to be blown up. The man admitted that the package contained a life-size female sex doll with an electronic device that vibrated and made "naughty" noises. The man said he was returning the doll to the manufacturer because it would spontaneously turn itself on at the most inopportune time—like in a post office. Postal authorities removed the batteries and sent the doll on her way. I hope they didn't send her third class—it would make her feel so cheap. ♥

While posing for an antique tintype photograph
and dressed in Old West–style clothing, a man
accidentally shot his wife with the rifle
he was using as a **prop**.

A Stiff Settlement

A Hong Kong man who claimed being hit by a motorcycle had diminished his sex life received a court settlement of $320,000. As part of the award, the man had earmarked $550 to purchase Viagra in order to overcome his handicap and to aid in his sexual healing. The man had originally demanded $5,500 worth of Viagra, enough for a ten-year supply, but the judge ruled there was no evidence to prove a ten-year treatment was necessary. Anyway, with $5,500 worth of Viagra he might not have lived for ten years. If he had, the coroner wouldn't have been able to get the smile off his face. ♥

A fifteen-year-old girl from Skokie, Illinois, became so angry with her eighteen-year-old boyfriend for not **kissing** her after the prom, she attacked him and **blackened** both of his eyes. She pleaded guilty to assault.

The Wall of Shame

A man in Rothenburg, Germany, was listed in critical condition after he fell into a garden from the top of a sixteen-foot wall. The story would hardly be noteworthy except for the fact that our Humpty Dumpty was completely naked. Apparently, and for some unknown reason, the man climbed to the top of the wall, took off all his clothes, and began taking photographs—of himself. Police aren't certain about the cause of the man's fall, but they're determined to get to the bottom of it even if it takes all the king's horses and all the king's men. ♥

Can You Repeat That?

adio station KSUB of Cedar City, Utah, was airing a feed of Mormon Church apostle M. Russell Ballard, who was preaching on the "pernicious evil" of the entertainment media. The station's digital buffer became overloaded by the data stream, causing Ballard's sermon to loop, or repeat, the last word over and over again until the buffer reset. So what the listening audience heard was Ballard saying the word "sex" repeatedly. "It was 'sex, sex, sex, sex, sex . . .' for twenty-four seconds," said KSUB's Dale Nelson. Surprisingly, the station didn't receive a single complaint from listeners. Either no one was listening to Ballard's sermon, or everyone took what he said to heart. ♥

Wedding Announcement

FINE-LOVEN

Jennifer Fine and Christopher Loven were married September 6, 1997, in Lionscrest Manor in Lyons by Gary Copeland.

Lost and Found

n Dennis, Massachusetts, a female police officer pulled over to the side of the road to assist a honeymooning couple who were lost. The officer gave directions, the woman driver thanked the officer, the officer got back into her patrol car and drove off—not much of a story so far, right? According to a police spokesman, "When the officer returned to the vehicle about ten minutes later, she saw the female hanging out of the car and the male jump on the female." The spokesman went on to say that the couple rolled onto the highway "punching each other." The officer arrested the lovebirds and charged them with mutual assault and disorderly conduct. Apparently they couldn't stay mad at each other long, because "they had an amorous reunion in the lobby of the police station, to the point where officers had to separate them again but in a different way." ♥

In Colorado:

"It is a misdemeanor for an acupuncturist to engage in sexual contact, and a felony to engage in sexual intrusion or penetration, with a patient during the course of patient care."

—Colorado Revised Statute §12-29.5-108 (enacted 1989)

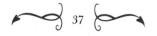

I Fall to Pieces

According to an article in the *Arizona Republic*, U.S. Marine James Glass, a victim of a grenade attack, was sent to a Kuwait hospital to convalesce. His injuries were the result of an attack, but not by the enemy one might expect—it was his wife, Wendy. "She has played the part of the dutiful wife, dutiful mother, all the while plotting the murder of . . . the father of her children," said prosecutor Sharon Sexton. For the past two years, Wendy had been having an affair with another Marine, and they confessed to plotting the murder so they could collect Glass's life insurance. You would think that after his wife tried to blow him up with a grenade, Glass's feelings for her would be shattered. According to defense attorney David Lee Titterington, however, "He considers their relationship, their marriage, in good standing. He stands beside her today." He probably doesn't stand beside her as much as lean beside her. ♥

CONCEIVING A WAY TO GET MORE BABIES

—*Sydney* (Australia) *Morning Herald*, March 3, 2005

The Way to a Man's Heart

osé Guadalupe "Lupe" Perez of San Antonio, Texas, and Beatriz, his wife of twenty-two years, had an argument. As usual, they soon made up. To make amends to her husband, Beatriz made him a sandwich that he lovingly accepted. After he ate the sandwich, Lupe felt terribly ill, and his daughter rushed him to the hospital. Beatriz admitted she poisoned the sandwich with the sedative Ativan because she was angry with her husband. "I ground up the pills and put them in Lupe's sandwich because I wanted to kill him," she told police. She confessed that this was the second time she had tried to kill Lupe; the first time she had only used three pills. "All he did was sleep all day." ♥

Pump You Up

A couple was fighting outside a Brooklyn, New York, nightclub over their six-year-old son when things got out of hand. The woman told her boyfriend she was going to marry someone else and the man "threatened to do something rash" if she didn't grant him visitation rights. The woman thought the man was acting like a real heel so she quickly took off her high heels and beat him with them. He later died from "multiple injuries, including chest compression and blunt trauma to the head, neck, and torso," a spokeswoman for the medical examiner said. The man had previously had his girlfriend charged with assault after an earlier fight, but he later dropped the charge. This is not a case of live and learn, but rather of learn and you'll live. ♥

In July 2001, Marie Solomon was arrested at a friend's wedding in Bridgeport, Connecticut, for relentlessly shouting out reasons why the couple should not wed.

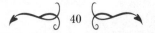

Wart Are You Looking At?

A Zambian woman gave her husband a piping hot cup of tea served in a special way, with a little sugar, a little milk, a little frog. It's unclear why Catherine Nyoka put the frog in her husband's tea, but one thing is sure—it made him hopping mad. So mad, in fact, that he leaped over to the local courthouse and filed for divorce. Nyoka claimed her husband was having an affair, but Andrew Nyoka said he wasn't attracted to other women until after his wife served him the toad tea. In September 2001, the court granted a divorce, stating the couple's marriage could not be saved. Andrew is now living with another woman and the love between him and his wife has simply croaked. ♥

The Quebec chapter of Hell's Angels was subdued by law enforcement agents after two bikers hired to be **contract killers** fell in love with each other. The love affair between Danny Boy Kane and Ace Simard was short lived; they cooperated with authorities, giving **crucial** information on the gang right after they broke up.

The Stamp of Approval

A man in Fallon, Nevada, received a thick, lumpy, envelope in the mail with no return address. He wasn't expecting a package, and having heard all the warnings about anthrax, he quickly called the sheriff's office. Deputies arrived and placed the suspicious package in a biohazard container while they investigated. It turns out the envelope didn't contain anything life threatening, but when the man saw the contents he began to shake and sweat, and his eyes popped out. Inside the envelope was a pair of ladies' black thong panties and a "sexually suggestive" letter. Authorities were able to trace the package back to the secret admirer who sent the lingerie-laced letter. "I feel kind of silly," the unidentified man said. "It just about blew my socks off." Maybe that's what the woman had in mind. ♥

Victorians assumed that even a glimpse of a **table leg** could incite a man to sexual **frenzy**, so they invented table skirts to prevent any **unnatural** unions between man and furniture.

—*The History of Sex,* the History Channel, August 1999

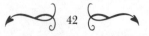

Bury Me Not on the Lone Prairie

n Sydney, Australia, a man was killed in a car accident, and his widow had his remains cremated. The bereaved woman had always kept her husband close to her heart, and she wanted that to continue. So she took his "cremains" and had them injected into her breast implants. According to the *Daily Star,* the twenty-six-year-old woman said, "It dawned on me that if I carried Dustin's cremated remains in my breast implants, I'd never really have to part with him at all." Dustin's dust in her bust, his final rest in her breast, certainly seems strange, but when it comes to a woman's love for her husband—you can't knock her. ♥

Fly the Friendly Skies

wo "noisy" frequent fliers disturbed passengers on an overnight British Airways flight from Phoenix, Arizona, to London, England. The couple, an American man and a British woman who were strangers before the flight, were taking full advantage of the fully reclining seats. After flight attendants asked the amorous couple to keep it down, they put everything in a fully upright and locked position and returned to their assigned seats. "We certainly would not encourage this sort of behavior," said a British Airways spokesman. "They obviously found our Club Class seats extremely comfortable." Or they just enjoyed flying United. ♥

PORTUGUESE SHEPHERD SHORT-CHANGED IN GOATS-FOR-WIFE DEAL

—Agence France-Presse headline, September 18, 2004

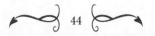

What's Cookin', Honey?

ell hath no fury like a woman scorned" is especially true if the woman scorned has a frying pan. A man in Tokyo, Japan, confessed to his wife that he was having an affair, and she quickly cooked up her revenge. She grabbed a frying pan and beat him with it. "You said you would die if you had an affair," the woman reminded him. "So I want you to die as you promised." Since his death wasn't panning out as quickly as she wanted, the woman took a kitchen knife and finished him off. At her trial in November 2001, the judge realized the woman's marriage was a tragic flash in the pan and sentenced her to only four years in prison. ♥

A forty-foot fishing boat, piloted by Suer Flemm of Finland, narrowly escaped the advances of a whale that attempted to have sex with it.

Finger-Licking Good

D ifferent cultures have different marriage customs. Some have a honeymoon, and others have a honey cup. In Iran, to have a sweet start on their marriage, an Iranian bride and groom dip their pinky fingers into a cup of honey and each feeds it to the other. Unfortunately, one Iranian bridegroom bit off more than he could chew and accidentally pulled off his bride's artificial nail. The nail got lodged in the man's throat, and no amount of slapping him on the back could get it to come up. The gagging groom collapsed and died on the spot, and the bride was rushed to the hospital after fainting from shock. Iranian law forbids a woman from filing a lawsuit, so even though she could point her finger at the company that made the faulty artificial nail, she couldn't sue it. ♥

In Florida:

"Whoever commits any unnatural and lascivious act with another person is guilty of a misdemeanor. A mother's breast-feeding of her baby does not violate this section."

—**Florida Statutes Annotated §800.02 (enacted 1993)**

A Fortune Nookie

A prostitute in Nagoya, Japan, has come up with a new trick for the oldest profession. The working girl, known only as Kaho, claims she can tell a man's future by having sex with him. And her soothsaying abilities go beyond "If your wife finds out you've had sex with a prostitute she'll kick your butt." Kaho, positioned in a brothel in Nagoya, claims she has predicted events for over a thousand men by performing oral sex on them. She takes credit for a man winning at a racetrack and encouraging a groom with cold feet to marry. Gives a unique slant on the phrase "Gaze into my crystal ball," doesn't it? ♥

A groom divorced his wife at their wedding reception in Riyadh, Saudi Arabia, after she had made fun of his mother's dancing ability.

How the Mighty Have Fallen

A Nicaraguan prisoner was enjoying a conjugal visit with his wife at a Mexican jail when the roof caved in, literally. The warden of the jail, Raul Zarate Díaz, was planning to spy on the couple when he tripped on a skylight, lost his balance, and crashed through the roof. The fall not only killed the couple's good time, it also killed the warden. *La Cronica* newspaper and InfoRed radio said the warden died when he hit the concrete floor; a pair of binoculars and a pornographic magazine were found on his body. Looks like the warden was doing a little self-imposed solitary confinement when things got out of hand. ♥

♥ ♥ ♥

Alan Leigh-Brown of Taunton,
England, purchased a DVD copy
of the 1957 Doris Day movie
The Pajama Game and was
shocked to see instead the
Italian film *Tettore che Passione*
("Breasts of Passion"). He was so
"horrified" and "shocked,"
according to Leigh-Brown, that
he felt obligated to watch
the entire film before returning it.

♥ ♥ ♥

Not Super Sex but Soup or Sex

ccording to a February 2002 article in the *Journal of Mundane Behavior* (no, I'm not making that up), a team of behavior specialists reported that boring sex has become a "global problem." Guest editor Kimberly Mahaffy, assistant professor of sociology at Millersville University of Pennsylvania, wrote that "mundane sex speaks to the 'truth' of our everyday experiences. The novelty and lust have been replaced by 'Can we do it before 10 P.M.?' 'Do I have to take my socks off?' 'Can I just lay here while you do the work'?" ♥

Passengers watched silently as John Henderson and Zoë D'Arcy engaged in oral sex and then moved on to intercourse on a jam-packed train from Margate to Victoria, England. But they were in a nonsmoking compartment, so as soon as the couple lit up **postcoital cigarettes**, a number of people complained.

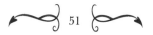

Oshkosh My Gosh

his kind of activity is not acceptable and we're not going to tolerate it," said outraged principal Rob Becker of Jefferson Elementary School in Oshkosh, Wisconsin. "This seems very much like sexual harassment in my opinion." Was the principal talking about a scandal involving two of his teachers? Nope, he was talking about the conduct of a six-year-old boy who tried to kiss a girl on the playground. The principal threatened that if this behavior was repeated, the boy would be suspended from school. I hope the young boy used the "Georgy Porgy, Pudding and Pie" defense. ♥

Every year, eleven thousand Americans injure themselves while trying out bizarre sexual positions.

I'll Keep an Eye Out for You

ocuments from a sexual harassment lawsuit against the management of a Safeway store in Kapolei, Hawaii, were a real eye-opener. In one incident, a female employee who realized she was being spied on thrust the handle of a toilet plunger through the peephole and into the peeper's eye socket. I don't think that was the "eyeful" he was hoping for. ♥

In New Jersey:

"Both parties must be eighteen to marry without parental approval. Sixteen- and seventeen-year-olds may marry with the consent of either parent; younger persons require both a parent's and judicial consent. An exception is made for a male under eighteen who has been arrested on a charge of sexual intercourse with a single, widowed, or divorced female of good repute for chastity who has thereby become pregnant; he does not need parental or judicial approval to marry her."

—New Jersey Statutes Annotated §37:1-6 (enacted 1977)

Three on a Match

Three strikes and you're out doesn't always relate to baseball. Case in point: Richard Levitt, of Wethersfield, Connecticut, thought it would be a good idea to videotape himself having sex with his girlfriend. Nothing really wrong with that, but, according to the *Hartford Courant,* Levitt decided to post the video on the Internet. Strike one was when the girlfriend found out. Strike two was when his other girlfriend found out. And strike three was when his wife found out. The best thing that happened to Mr. Levitt was his arrest for disseminating voyeuristic materials. How was that the best thing? It got him away from three very angry women. For him it wasn't a matter of three strikes and you're out; he was afraid of two balls with three errors. ♥

MAN ON WAY TO BROTHEL FINDS WIFE WORKING

—Reuters headline, January 25, 2001

This Ain't Mr. Rogers' Neighborhood

A Romanian man filed a lawsuit against his neighbors seeking nearly $12,000 in damages. Neculai Olaru, seventy-two, claimed he was unable to rest in his apartment in Bucharest because of the continuous sound of lovemaking emanating from his neighbors' apartment. "They start as soon as they arrive home at 6 P.M. I thought I would get some peace after they finished, but they just start again and again. I didn't scream like that when I was their age," Mr. Olaru said. Since he wasn't able to sleep, Mr. Olaru claimed his health declined, which eventually led to a heart attack. I wonder if the couple next door heard the moans and groans of Mr. Olaru having a heart attack and thought he was joining in on the fun. ♥

Come On, Baby, Light My Fire

A Romanian man got his girlfriend so hot she had to be taken to the hospital. Bogdan Radovan and his girlfriend, Alina Munteanu, had finished making love in his car at a local lovers' lane in Balcesti, County Vulcea, and he lighted up a postcoital cigarette. After he took the last puff, Radovan threw the still burning butt out the window. The cigarette ignited some brush, and soon there was a sizable fire next to their car. Still naked, Ms. Munteanu jumped out of the car and tried to put out the flames with a blanket. The woman got burned on her bottom, Mr. Radovan made an emergency call on his cell phone, they were rescued by firefighters, and Ms. Munteanu was taken to the hospital. This is a classic case of a burning butt causing a burning butt. ♥

"Insanity is not evidenced when a widow, anxious to marry, shows her love letters from one suitor to another, and boasts constantly about her conquests, both real and those imagined."

—Oklahoma common law

Nothing Will Ever Come Between Us

fter a bitter divorce, former couples will inevitably build a wall between each other. Janet O'Hara took that metaphor and put real bricks and mortar to it. Janet and Bill Vernon divorced after ten years, and their settlement gave Janet the riding stables and Bill the adjoining farm. Bill converted an annex to be rented out, and the building backed onto the stable property. Mrs. O'Hara was tired of seeing her former husband coming onto her land to maintain the new property, so she built a six-foot-high, thirty-foot-long wall two inches from his back door. Bill Vernon complained that the wall was so close he couldn't open the back door, and he was forced to leave the lights on all day, as the wall blocked the sun. But the law is on her side, and Bill must stay on his side. If he tries to tear down or even deface the wall, he will immediately be charged with criminal damage. Now that the courts have ruled in her favor, I'm sure Mrs. O'Hara can refer to her wall as an obstruction of justice. ♥

♥ ♥ ♥

In Charleston, West Virginia, police arrested Joey Armstrong on charges of trespassing, destruction of property, and cruelty to animals. Armstrong apparently broke into a shed used to house animals for a live nativity scene at the Bartlett-Burdette-Cox Funeral Home and raped a sheep.

♥ ♥ ♥

It's a Dog's Life

Tricia Parker was taking her fifteen-year-old Labrador, Laddie, for a walk when the old dog wanted a new trick. He spied a female dog across the street, and the Lab broke free of his mistress and darted after the female he'd spotted. "He saw this other dog and he was off, but he collapsed before he got to her. He has a leaky valve in his heart, and he got so excited his heart stopped," Tricia told the *Lancashire* (England) *Evening Post*. Fortunately for her, and the dog, Paul Whalley was out walking his dog when he saw the old Lab collapse. He quickly went over to the Lab, assessed the situation, and performed mouth to snout resuscitation, which saved the dog's life. The female dog, which obviously wasn't into what appeared to be bispecies sex, left the scene. ♥

According to an article in the *Thanh Nien* ("Young People") newspaper, reported by Reuters, a Vietnamese woman who couldn't convince her husband to give up an affair with a younger woman agreed to **sell him** to her for $516.

Driving on the Parkway and Parking on the Driveway

According to West Rockhill Township (Pennsylvania) authorities, Evelyn Torress and Daniel Villafane were apparently traveling from Allentown to the Philadelphia area shortly after 7 A.M. on February 24, 2002, when they decided, for some reason, to pull into a stranger's driveway near the Route 309 exit ramp and have sex. Neighbors saw the couple inside the car, and then watched as they jumped out and did the bump and grind on the trunk. Police were dispatched, and when they arrived, the couple were dressed and innocently seated in the front seat of the red Dodge Neon. While Sergeant Rodney Blake questioned the two about their impromptu pit stop, he detected the smell of marijuana, and then noticed an opened cigar box on the passenger-side floorboard containing six bags of pot. A search warrant turned up another larger bag of marijuana in the backseat. All in all the couple were caught with more than two pounds of marijuana, packaged in over four hundred sandwich bags, with a street value of about $11,000. Their joint venture, and I mean that several different ways, will keep them in the joint for a long time. ♥

♥ ♥ ♥

As the organist hadn't
shown up for the wedding of
Tracey Muxworthy, a guest
at the ceremony played the
tinny strains of "Here Comes
the Bride" on his cellular phone.

—Aberdare, Wales, October 2002

♥ ♥ ♥

Rollin' on the River

couple parked by the River Enns near the city of Graz, Austria, and went skinny-dipping—by accident. The unidentified man and woman had been making love for about fifteen minutes when they suddenly felt the car moving. The hand brake wasn't set properly, and the car rolled down an embankment and into the icy river, where it sank. The pair quickly uncoupled, escaped from inside the vehicle, and swam unharmed to the riverbank. ♥

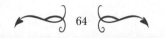

Instead of being hit by rice, one bride from Zonguldak, Turkey, was hit by pellets from an air rifle. The ballistic bride, Aynur Tayoglu, was taken to the hospital to remove several pellets lodged in her stomach. Her future father-in-law refused to reschedule the wedding, saying too many relatives had traveled a long way, and he wasn't going to disappoint them. The doctors agreed to postpone surgery, and Tayoglu returned to complete the ceremony and, despite her wounds, danced at her own wedding.

Ability or Disability?

ntonio Contreras took his case against Suncast
Corporation of Illinois all the way to the U.S. Supreme
Court, where his appeal was eventually turned down.
Contreras had sued under the Americans with Disabilities Act
claiming he was fired as a forklift operator although he had a sexual
dysfunction, which is a federally protected disability. Court
documents showed that Contreras sought damages against the
company on the grounds that he used to have sex five times a week,
but an injury limited him to twice a month, and that's the reason the
company fired him. ♥

LOVERS' PASSIONATE PIT STOP
SENDS CAR OFF CLIFF IN ARGENTINA

—Agence France-Presse headline, October 20, 2004

One in the Hand

A twenty-three-year-old man from Madrid, Spain, was out on the town with his girlfriend and thought he was going to get lucky. He stopped by a condom machine outside a pharmacy, put in the coins, pulled the plunger, and nothing happened. The man pounded on the machine trying to loosen the condom package, but it would not budge. Noticing the spontaneity of the moment quickly slipping by, he slipped his hand into the slot and immediately got two of his fingers caught. Try as he might, he couldn't get his fingers out, and he was forced to stand there for four hours, becoming the brunt of humiliating comments from passersby, until help arrived and freed his fingers. It wasn't reported if the man ever got his condoms or not, but it's a sure thing that his fingers were the only things that got tugged on that night. ♥

In Indiana:

"A person living in adultery receives no part of a deceased spouse's estate."

—Indiana Code §29-1-2-14 (enacted 1953)

A Display of Passion

A burglar alarm summoned police to a western boot store in Bakersfield, California. When police passed in front of the large display window, they noticed there was more in there than just hand-tooled leather boots. There was a naked couple that had gone from hand-tooled to knocking boots. An officer tapped on the window to alert the two booty-bouncing burglars that they were getting the boot. The couple took to their heels but were quickly apprehended and charged with burglary, resisting arrest, assaulting an officer, and indecent exposure. The two bootlicks admitted they had broken into the store to get out of the rain and then ducked into a "hidden" place to have sex. If the shoe fits, wear it—but if the boot fits, wear it out. ♥

Nebraska state trooper Sam Winters pulled over a young man in Banner County who explained, "Officer, I have a **hot date** tonight in Scottsbluff, and if you'd seen this girl, **you'd be speeding, too.**"

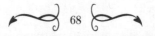

Something Borrowed, Something Blue

A couple from Moundsville, West Virginia, thought it would be romantic to have their wedding on Valentine's Day. With butterflies in their stomachs, Denise Lynn Rose and Luigi Louis Corvino Sr. appeared at the Marshall County Courthouse ready to take their vows. But instead of a best man, a sheriff's deputy showed up and arrested the couple. The sheriff's department received a tip when the couple's names appeared on the family court judge's docket. The two had previously been arrested on charges of domestic battery against each other, and as a condition of their bond, they were banned from having any contact with each other. So it wasn't "until death do us part"; it was "until deputies do us part." ♥

Romanian man, known only as Todrut, was determined to marry a woman with the same name as his dead wife, Lorelei. He told a newspaper reporter: "The woman with whom I am going to spend the rest of my life will be called Lorelei. And this is because I want to remember my first love and all that was beautiful in my life." The name Lorelei is not a common one in Romania.

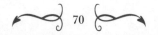

Being Ungroomed

he bride and groom were in the middle of exchanging wedding vows in Mafikeng, South Africa, when officials intervened and stopped the wedding. Were they responding to the preacher's question, "If anyone knows a reason why this couple shouldn't be married, speak now or forever hold your peace"? No, they stopped the wedding because the groom was a woman. Well, the groom wasn't really a woman, but his birth certificate had him listed as a female. According to the *Citizen* newspaper, the couple had to postpone the wedding indefinitely until the groom, Randoa Molefe, had doctor's proof that he was a man. I bet he was planning on proving this fact on his wedding night. ♥

Nicolae Popa, who runs a food distribution company in Alba Lulia, Romania, made a deal with his wife, Maria. He pays her $575 a month—and she promises not to **nag** him.

Getting the Bird

A Chinese housewife from the Chongquing Province filed for divorce on the grounds that her husband was having an affair. The woman claimed she received proof of the affair when a little bird told her. Upon returning from a month-long visit with her parents, the woman became suspicious because every time the phone rang, her mynah bird spouted phrases like "Divorce," "I love you," and "Be patient." ♥

"Every person who shall seduce and have sexual intercourse with any female of previously chaste character shall be punished by imprisonment in the state penitentiary for not more than five (5) years or in the county jail for not more than one (1) year or by a fine of $1000 or by both fine and imprisonment."

—An Auburn, Washington, law

Till Death Do Us Part—
or at Least Do You Part

I thought I had seen every way to steal, scam, or con people out of money, but it's hard to believe someone would do this," a police detective said. The detective was talking about the charming Robert Meier of Tampa, Florida, who forged a license to "marry" his comatose girlfriend before she died. Was he a hopeless romantic fulfilling his girlfriend's last wishes? Nope. He used the forged marriage license so he could use her credit card, with which he ran up more than $20,000 in charges before he was caught. During the investigation, Meier claimed the woman's dog told him to do it. A theory I doubt, as the man didn't use the credit card to buy a lifetime supply of dog biscuits or to purchase a couple of twin female poodles. ♥

A Hunka, Hunka Burnin' Love

A love-struck man will go to just about any extreme to impress the woman of his dreams. An arsonist who appeared before a female judge in Vienna, Austria, was so smitten with her that, after she released him on bail, he asked her out on a date. The judge refused, but that didn't quench the fire in the man's heart. He had a burning desire to see her again, so he started burning more things. The admitted arsonist confessed that his plan was to continue setting fires so he could appear before the female judge again. It worked. She sentenced him to two years in prison. Now that's hot. ♥

In Michigan:

"A woman shall not marry her father, brother, grandfather, son, grandson, stepfather, grandmother's husband, daughter's husband, granddaughter's husband, husband's father, husband's grandfather, husband's son, husband's grandson, brother's son, sister's son, father's brother, mother's brother, or cousin of the first degree, or another woman."

—**Michigan Penal Code, Revised Statutes of 1846 (Chapter 83, 551.4.)**

I'll Take a Stab at It

Stephen Nash told his wife, Michelle, their marriage was over, and he wanted a divorce. After the emotional breakup, Stephen went off to bed, and when he woke up later, he had a sharp pain in his side. The cause of the pain was quickly identified when Stephen noticed a knife was curiously sticking out of his body. During her trial for attempted murder, the prosecution, of course, contended that Michelle had tried to stab her husband to death. But the defense had a story that was more cutting edge: Stephen had stabbed himself while having a nightmare. The jury plunged into the stabbing case and believed Michelle was telling the truth, and the judge cut her loose. ♥

VATICAN SEX GUIDE URGES CATHOLICS TO DO "IT" MORE OFTEN

—*London Telegraph,* October 31, 2004

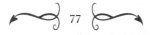

Unchained Melody

erry Thomason, of San Antonio, Texas, loved his wife so much that he was charged with aggravated assault. In April 2003, the forty-one-year-old man was arrested after it was discovered that he kept his wife from leaving him by locking a heavy chain around her neck and attaching it to the floor. Witnesses claimed that Thomason loved his wife but was always afraid she was going to try and leave him. Duh? ♥

A German couple demanded **$4,000** in damages from a tour operator because the maid at their hotel walked in on them **twice** while they were having sex, even though they had a DO NOT DISTURB sign hung on the door.

A Little Trim

ighteen-year-old Justine Hayes-Hurley and sixteen-year-old Lisandro Mateo of Central Islip, New York, were charged with criminal mischief in March 2003 after they vandalized a car. While discussing their love lives, the girls realized they had something in common—a boyfriend. They went looking for twenty-year-old, two-timing Winston Hill, and fortunately for him, they came across his car first. Since the boyfriend left such an impression on both girls, they thought they would leave an impression on his car with a pair of hedge clippers. It was shear luck that Winston's twig and berries didn't get a different kind of trim. ♥

The Wind Beneath My Wings

he groom wore a donated tuxedo and stood nervously and unsteadily next to his bride, who was all in white. Sounds like a typical wedding except the bride's white wasn't a dress—it was bandages that covered her broken foot, her two broken arms, and other injuries. Jimmi Langley and Ronnie Ray, both eighteen, of Harriman, Tennessee, had survived a deadly tornado that swept through their mountain community on Sunday, November 10, 2002. They had planned to marry that week, but not in the intensive care unit at the Roane Medical Center. However, their love was stronger than the wind, and when the Reverend Stewart Slone, pastor of their Church of God of Prophecy in Petros, asked Jimmi, "Will you love him, comfort him, honor and keep him in sickness and in health . . . so long as you both shall live?" she could have answered, "I already have," but the simple "I do" did the trick. ♥

A man in Hazard, Kentucky, divorced his wife because she "beat him whenever he removed onions from his hamburgers without first asking for permission."

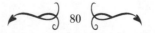

That Was Summit Mistake

iamonds may be forever but this one particular gem may be forever lost. Climbing to new heights on the list of unique proposals, a couple hiked twelve thousand feet to the top of South Bowl at Keystone Resort, where Derek Monnig dropped to one knee. Unfortunately, the next thing he did was drop a 1.25-carat diamond and platinum engagement ring valued at $6,500 into a foot of freshly fallen snow. The ring was meant for the finger of Debra Sweeney. "He said, 'I have something for you. Honey, I love you. Will you marry me?'" Sweeney remembered. "He pulled this box out, opened it up, went to put the ring on my finger—and it dropped. It was horrible." Sweeney stayed motionless for fifteen minutes while Monnig dug through the snow, to no avail. He climbed back to the summit the next day with a metal detector but came down empty-handed. Sweeney didn't go empty-handed for long, however, as the ring was fully insured. Having this bungled betrothal happen at Keystone Resort is almost too funny to be true. ♥

A Great Dane

This is the kind of frozen Danish you won't find in your freezer. A Danish man from Horsens, the Netherlands, was spotted by a neighbor shivering on the frozen roof of his girlfriend's house. The man and his girlfriend were engaged in a romantic encounter on a February night in 2003 when they heard the woman's husband coming home. The man, who was naked, by the way, climbed out of the bedroom window and stayed there for two hours, until officers arrived and coaxed him down. By that time he really was a Danish with frosting. ♥

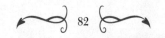

Buttocks: The area at the rear of the human body (sometimes referred to as the glutaeus maximus) which lies between two imaginary straight lines running parallel to the ground when a person is standing, the first or top such line being ½-inch below the top of the vertical cleavage of the nates (i.e., the prominence formed by the muscles running from the back of the hip to the back of the leg) and the second or bottom such line being ½-inch above the lowest point of the curvature of the fleshy protuberance (sometimes referred to as the gluteal fold), and between two imaginary straight lines, one on each side of the body (the "outside line"), which outside lines are perpendicular to the ground and to the horizontal lines described above and which perpendicular outside lines pass through the outermost point(s) at which each nate meets the outer side of each leg. Notwithstanding the above, Buttocks shall not include the leg, the hamstring muscle below the gluteal fold, the tensor fasciae latae muscle or any of the above-described portion of the human body that is between either (i) the left inside perpendicular line and the left outside perpendicular line or (ii) the right inside perpendicular line and the right outside perpendicular line.. . .

—Part of Public Nudity Ordinance 92-12, Section 3, passed and adopted by the Board of County Commissioners of St. Johns County, State of Florida, April 21, 1992

Can You Hear Me Now?

While in his car having sex with his mistress, a Finnish man inadvertently hit a speed-dial button on his cell phone. The call reached out and touched someone, all right—unfortunately, that someone was the man's wife. She picked up the receiver just in time to hear the other woman moan, "I love you." The enraged wife didn't need caller ID because she recognized the voice as that of a close friend. The wronged woman let her fingers do the walking, went to her ex-friend's house, and struck her in the face. Still having an ax to grind with her husband, she was later arrested, had the ax taken from her, and convicted of assault. ♥

An August 2001 *Journal of Sex Research* report by two Georgia State University professors concluded that people who want sex but are not getting any are **grumpier** than those who are having sex or even those who don't desire it.

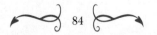

Going Off Half-Cocked

A Sicilian man was admitted to a hospital in the city of Piazza Armerina with a shotgun wound to the groin. At first, the man claimed the damage was the result of a hunting accident, but before the pellets came out, the truth was revealed. The man had asked one of his friends to shoot him in the groin in the hope that his ex-girlfriend would feel sorry for him. I've heard of shooting your mouth off to get attention, but this is ridiculous! ♥

The largest wedding cake ever (according to *Guinness World Records 2005: Special 50th Anniversary Edition*) weighed **15,032 pounds** and was made by the chefs at the Mohegan Sun Hotel and Casino in Uncasville, Connecticut, for their New England bridal showcase on February 8, 2004.

Tommy, Can You Hear Me?

ella Drimland of Denver, Colorado, filed for divorce after realizing her husband of seven years had been lying to her. Did he have an affair? No, he had been pretending for the last several years to be deaf and dumb. Bill Drimland admitted that he adopted the Helen Keller routine to escape his wife's endless nagging. He thought she would stop her incessant ragging once he turned deaf, but when that didn't work, he decided to become mute as well. I guess she wasn't too bad to look at or else he would have faked being blind, too. ♥

♥ ♥ ♥

Sharon Kirkman of Panama City, Florida, lost her home after an argument with her husband. She didn't lose it in a divorce— she lost it after she became livid with her husband and set fire to one of his shirts. The fire spread and burned the house down. Insurance adjusters said they wouldn't cover the damage because the fire was set by one of the owners.

♥ ♥ ♥

Field of Dreams

hris Mueller of Hillsboro, North Dakota, is in a field of his own when it comes to proposing. Mueller was on his tractor in his bean field when he decided to write a message to his girlfriend, Katie Goltz. So he plowed the field intending to spell out the message *"Katie, will you marry me?"* He was nearly finished when he noticed he was quickly running out of room in the field, so he had to make a decision. He knew he couldn't erase what he had already written, so he purposely left an "r" out of "marry." When he took his girlfriend for a plane ride over the field, she didn't notice the misspelling at first, since her eyes were too filled with tears of joy. When she realized that the word "marry" was misspelled, she said, "I thought it was so sweet that he spelled it wrong. I thought it made it more cute and more special." The roots of Chris's proposal go back to his father, Tom Mueller, who has fielded two romantic messages to his wife, Diane. When they were engaged, he plowed a heart with Diane's name in it, and on their twenty-fifth wedding anniversary, he sowed a "no. 25" into a bean field. For father and son Mueller, plowing the fields has always been a labor of love. ♥

Second Verse, Same as the First

Keith Chesterfield must either love history or love Herman's Hermits. For the man's sixth wedding he and his future bride thought it would be fun to have a theme wedding. "I have always been fascinated by history and when Paige [Bell] suggested we do something a bit different to mark the big day, this seemed like a great idea," he said. "It just seemed fitting that we should base it on Henry VIII as he had six wives as well," Bell chimed in. I'm not sure why the bride didn't lose her head over the idea, as the chronology of Henry VIII's wives goes like this: He divorced the first one, had the second one executed, the third one died, he divorced the fourth one, the fifth one was executed, and the sixth one outlived him. ♥

Attila the Hun died on his wedding night in A.D. 453 from a severe nosebleed.

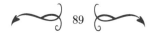

It's the Thought That Counts

While sitting in his jail cell in Dilley, Texas, Hermilo Mendez, realized he finally had the time to work on his long overdue divorce. He wrote the county clerk in San Antonio in March 2002 to begin the process, but noted that there was one small problem—he couldn't remember his wife's name. Mendez recalled that he met the girl of his dreams ten years earlier in 1992 and after a one-week romance got married. Eight days as man and wife had obviously turned the dream into a nightmare, and the woman packed her bags and left. The clerk eventually shook the man's matrimonial memory by uncovering the documents that identified his backdated better half as Violeta Sanchez Juarez. She had moved back to Mexico years ago. ♥

YOU CAN'T BUY LOVE, BUT EURO BRINGS CHEAPER SEX

—Reuters headline, January 1, 2002

I Smell a Rat

A postman from London, England, filed for divorce because his wife of thirty-four years continually insisted they share their bed with two others. The woman wasn't demanding that she and her husband engage in a ménage-à-quatre—she just refused to sleep without her two pet ferrets. The husband complained that the smelly rodents were a nuisance in bed and that his wife spent more time with them than she did with him. He filed on the grounds of unreasonable behavior. Maybe the husband should have ferreted out the real source of his wife's passive-aggressive behavior before he tried to weasel out of their marriage. ♥

A Stockport, England, environmental officer received
so many noise complaints that he publicly urged citizens
to be more quiet at night while having sex.
Obviously, he didn't use the phrase **"Keep it down."**

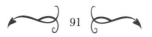

Size Does Matter

A young Sri Lankan woman began an affair with a coworker, and after a brief courtship, they married in a secret ceremony. The bride had very strict parents, so the couple lived separately for three months before finally getting a house of their own. On the day they moved in, the bride's parents came to their new home and forcibly took back their daughter. The groom stormed over to his in-laws' house to retrieve his wife, when the parents noticed something their daughter had overlooked—her husband was a woman. The parents became suspicious about the groom's mannerisms or womannerisms, confronted their something-in-law, and the female groom confessed. The young bride asked a Colombo, Sri Lanka, court to nullify the marriage based on the grounds that she was deceived. She claimed the deception negatively affected her job performance and her education. The truth is she probably didn't want to share her clothes with her husband. ♥

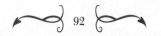

In North Carolina:

"It is (also) a misdemeanor for any man and woman to be found occupying the same bedroom in any hotel, public inn, or boardinghouse for any immoral purpose, or for any man and woman to falsely register as, or otherwise represent themselves to be, husband and wife in any hotel, public inn, or boardinghouse."

—**North Carolina General Statute §14-186 (enacted 1917)**

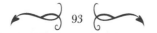

The Sound of Silence

en in Muslim Yemen can marry up to four wives and are allowed to divorce any or all without giving a reason. According to the *Al-Thawra* newspaper, a man named Yahya from the southern Dhamar Province of Yemen divorced his first wife but did give a reason; it was because of her constant nagging and arguing. The forty-year-old man said that after fifteen years he was tired of his wife's "screaming and endless disputes" and had his sights set on a new bride. The man's new wife, the paper reported, is quiet and mild-mannered mainly because "he chose one deprived of hearing and speech." ♥

She was cursing like a sailor," a South Windsor, Connecticut, police spokesman said of the intoxicated and out-of-control bride, Adrienne Samen. Samen was arrested and taken to police headquarters still wearing her wedding dress after creating a public disturbance by throwing cake and flower vases and verbally assaulting her new husband, a Marine who had recently returned from Iraq. She allegedly tried to bite police officers in the police booking room, and she threw her wedding ring so hard it bent.

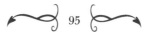

A Clear and Present Danger

athryn Marie Patrick received one wedding gift she wasn't expecting—a $5,000 bail bond. The bride was taken into custody after flinging wedding cake at her husband, punching him in the face, and then kicking him as he tried to crawl to cover. Police reported that the woman became enraged while arguing with her husband about wedding gifts. I can hear it now: "If we get one more toaster, I'm going to snap." ♥

Joseph Bisignano of Des Moines, Iowa, sued his long-sought-after girlfriend, Mary Toon, for fraud, breach of contract, and "unjust enrichment" in January 2003. The suit demanded reimbursement in the amount of $129,000 for gifts and $201,259 cash for loans and purchases. In order to win her over as his fourth bride, Bisignano bought Toon a $75,000 engagement ring, a designer wedding dress, and a $4,000 fur coat before she dumped him.

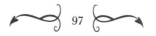

The Daily Double

It was just hours before their son's wedding when a Romanian family received the horrible news that their son had been in a serious car accident and was now in a coma. The Carasel family from the village of Turceni, Romania, had planned for an extremely expensive wedding for their son and decided they only had one choice—the wedding must go on—so they had to find a stand-in. Dumitru Carasel took the place of his comatose brother, Gabriel, saying, "Gabriel will marry his bride when he recovers, until then we should celebrate." It was not reported whether the brother only stood in for the wedding service or if he conducted other services, as well. ♥

The Bride Wore Black

An undertaker, Margaret Cullen, wore a gothic black dress as she walked down the aisle at Strone Church in Dunoon Argyll, Scotland. She arrived in a hearse for the occasion, but the occasion wasn't a funeral—it was her wedding. "Undertaking provided us with a great deal of satisfaction and that is why we chose to have a funeral theme," she told the *Daily Record*. The theme included a coffin-shaped wedding cake. The groom in this ghoulish get-together was former undertaker Carl Evans. "A lot of our guests are also connected with funerals, and I think they appreciated the gesture we made," said the macabre Mrs. Evans. I wonder if the preacher became confused during the "until death do you part" line. ♥

A fifty-two-year-old woman from the Italian town of Chieti divorced her ninety-four-year-old husband after only five months because he demanded too much sex.

A Real Mail-Order Bride

Brazilian man was so incensed when his parents demanded that he divorce his wife that he went on a killing spree. While arguing with her son over his choice of a bride, the seventy-one-year-old mother grabbed a pair of scissors and lunged at the man's "wife." He wrestled the scissors from her hands, and while his wife sat there emotionlessly, he murdered both his mother and his seventy-year-old father. Police said the man acted in a fit of passionate rage and admitted that his wife was a real doll. That is, she was a real doll. The unemployed man "thought the doll was a human being, called her his bride, and talked to her," a family acquaintance said. The man was taken to jail and needless to say, his wife was utterly deflated. ♥

CLINTON APOLOGIZES TO SYPHILIS VICTIMS

—Associated Press headline, May 16, 1997

♥ ♥ ♥

According to the police in
New Albany, Indiana,
Charles Adams convinced his
friend Clifton "Scooter" Foster
to stab him because Adams
wanted to see if his ex-girlfriend
would visit him in the hospital.

♥ ♥ ♥

Sooner or Later

A couple from Cliftonville, England, spent two years and thousands of dollars planning a round-the-world trip for their twenty-fifth wedding anniversary. Barry and Carol Watson had a mountain of information to coordinate, so it's understandable that they might overlook one insignificant detail—and they did. But the detail they got wrong was the date of their twenty-fifth anniversary; they scheduled everything a year too early. While on their twenty-fifth anniversary round-the-world trip, they were too embarrassed to tell their hosts about their mistake, but not too embarrassed to give back all the gifts. ♥

Anthony Comstock (1844–1915), a morality crusader in the late nineteenth and early twentieth centuries, supervised the destruction of more than 800,000 "**obscene**" pictures and more than 98,000 stories that dealt with the "**immoral**" use of rubber."

—*The History of Sex,* the History Channel, August 1999

They Put the "Nut" in "Doughnut"

ick Skalkos was celebrating his twenty-fifth birthday with his girlfriend, Sarah LeRiche, and twenty of his friends in a doughnut shop in Kitchener, Ontario, Canada. Dressed in jeans, shorts, and running shoes, Nick casually told Sarah that he loved her. The jelly-filled doughnuts must have gone to his head because when a friend asked when they were going to get married, Nick, with a glazed look in his eyes, surprised everyone. He grabbed his honey bun and asked one of their guests, the Reverend Frank Quinto, if he would perform the marriage ceremony right there. Even though the minister said it was the "weirdest wedding" he'd ever been to, it was perfectly legal. I wonder if the guests threw sprinkles instead of rice? Maybe the groom went all out on the ring and got her a chocolate glaze instead of the plain cake one! ♥

Scent of a Woman

Lynda Taylor was charged with aggravated battery after she allegedly assaulted her husband's sense of smell. David Taylor is fragrance-sensitive, and he became disoriented and unable to call for help after his wife assailed him by dousing herself heavily with perfume, plugging in dozens of scented air fresheners and lighting scented candles, and emptying lavender-scented sachets and sprinkling them throughout the house. Taylor said that right after he and his wife discussed separating, the air became so thick you could cut it with a knife. ♥

ean McNulty was at the Houston airport preparing to board a plane that would take him and his wife to a romantic honeymoon destination. He left his wife at the terminal to retrieve his forgotten wallet from his car, but he never returned to her. Three days later, McNulty was discovered in a hospital near the airport suffering from amnesia following a blow to the head. He didn't remember the wedding, his bride, or even going to the airport. His wife has been working with him in the hope of jogging his memory.

Going to the Doghouse

A divorced man in Alicante, Spain, appeared in court and pleaded with the judge to allow him visitation rights to his seven-year-old, and the judge acquiesced. Now every weekend the man can go to his former wife's house and visit his beloved seven-year-old poodle. The ex–husband and wife agreed to share custody of the animal "for the good of the dog," the man's lawyer said. Maybe if the man had spent more time rubbing his wife's belly and scratching her behind the ear, then she might not have treated him like a dog. ♥

In Georgia:

"An unmarried person commits the offense of fornication when he voluntarily has sexual intercourse with another person and, upon conviction thereof, shall be punished as for a misdemeanor."

—**Official Code of Georgia Annotated §§ 16-6-18 (enacted 1833)**

Prisoner of Love

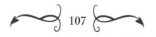n Italian prisoner was given a seventy-two-hour leave for good behavior and went straight from the Vigevano Prison into the open arms of his wife. A jailer was surprised when, only a few minutes after the man left, he received a call from the prisoner begging to come back. "He said he couldn't stand being with his wife and was it possible to go back to his cell. He said he didn't want to spend another minute with her," a spokesman for the jail said. Iron bars do not a prison make. ♥

A woman in Hardwick, Georgia, divorced her husband on the grounds that he "stayed home too much and was **much too affectionate**."

Birds of a Feather

t's the thought that counts" is what I'm sure one Minnesota man is still saying to his wife. Bill Fickett of St. Cloud thought he would be a considerate husband and relieve his wife of the task of cooking the Thanksgiving bird. He filled his turkey deep-fryer up with canola oil, turned it on, and went inside to get the turkey. Bill strutted into the kitchen feeling like the cock-of-the-walk, but soon he had to gobble his pride when the garage burst into flames. The turkey deep-fryer had caught fire and Bill was soon plucked out of $14,000 in repair costs. After he got a dressing down from his wife, he remarked, "I'll probably stick to baking them." ♥

The Good, the Bad, and the Ugly

Mr. Jian Feng, of Hegang in northern China, became suspicious of his wife's faithfulness when she gave birth to what he considered to be a seriously ugly baby. Knowing that he was a handsome man, Mr. Feng confronted his beautiful wife and accused her of adultery. Mrs. Feng promised that the baby was his and that she had been absolutely faithful, as far as her marital fidelity was concerned, but not about her looks. The now exquisite Mrs. Feng admitted she used to be excruciatingly ugly and that before they met, she had extensive plastic and reconstructive surgery in South Korea. Mr. Feng took his ugly baby home and took his beautiful wife to court, divorced her, and a few months later sued her for fraud. And that was the story of the good, the bad, and the ugly. It was *good* that she told him the truth. It was *bad* that he left her anyway. And, damn, that's one *ugly* baby! ♥

♥ ♥ ♥

A Swedish man in prison on a drug conviction was allowed a weekend release but failed to show up after the leave was over. According to the Swedish daily *Aftonbladet,* police caught the man at his own wedding, allowed him to marry his bride, but then whisked him up the aisle and back to prison, thus denying him his honeymoon. Now that's cruel and unusual punishment.

♥ ♥ ♥

Oh, Canada

A survey conducted in September 2005 by JWT Worldwide, a New York–based ad agency, asked 2,126 English-speaking men and women in the United States, Britain, Canada, and the Netherlands a series of questions regarding sex. And unfortunately, Canada ranks number one in terms of female sexual satisfaction. Of the 1,034 participating Canadians, 43 percent of the women said "sex is overrated" and 29 percent of the men agreed with the statement. ♥

In Delaware:

"A man forfeits all demands on his wife's estate by leaving his wife to be with an adulteress or by living in adultery separated from his wife if the conduct is not occasioned by the wife's fault and the wife does not permit the husband to dwell with her after the offense."

—Delaware Code Annotated Title 25 §744 (enacted 1935)

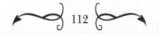

Ships That Cross in the Night

Sitting alone in his apartment in Sydney, Australia, Ian Johnstone missed his girlfriend so much that he hopped on a plane and flew back to London to surprise her and propose to her. His girlfriend, Amy Dolby, sitting in her apartment in London, missed Ian, too, and wanting to surprise him, got on a flight to Sydney. Both planes were in the air at the same time flying in opposite directions and both had a layover and connecting flight in Singapore. Ian and Amy unknowingly sat in the same airport lounge on that particular day in July 2001 only a short distance from each other while waiting for their connecting flights. Dolby excitedly knocked on the door of Johnstone's Sydney apartment after her exhausting eleven-thousand-mile flight anxious to see the surprised look in his eyes. Johnstone's roommate opened the door and was very surprised to see Dolby standing there when he knew that Johnstone had just flown to London to be with her. At that exact moment, Johnstone, armed with an engagement ring, champagne, and flowers was knocking on the door of Dolby's empty apartment. He thought she was pulling his leg when she called him on the phone and said she was in Sydney. Soon the cruel irony of the situation became apparent. He decided to make the best of the situation and since he had the ring, the champagne, and the flowers already, he asked Dolby to marry him. She accepted. She told him to stay put, got on the next plane back to England, and eventually flew into his arms. ♥

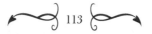

There She Blows

magine the surprise of dozens of beach goers out for a relaxing day at Mentor Headlands State Park Beach on Lake Erie near Cleveland, Ohio. They unfolded their blankets, got out their picnic baskets, and checked out the beautiful surroundings: the beach, the sparkling waters of the lake, the couple having sex. Apparently, Jim Santoro and Judith Reichel were bobbing up and down, but they weren't in the water. Several families complained to lifeguards, and the couple was arrested and hauled into the courtroom of Painesville judge Michael Cicconetti. The judge gave the couple a choice—they could either go to jail for twenty-two days for public indecency or they could each make a public apology. He ordered them to publish ads in two local newspapers, with the wording "I apologize for any activities that I engaged in that were offensive and disrespectful." I'm sure the ads about their June 13, 2002, tryst will be an interesting addition to the couple's scrapbook and will make for a great conversation starter. ♥

♥ ♥ ♥

A couple making out
at a Loudon County, Virginia,
lovers' lane became so nervous
when they saw a sheriff's car
drive up that the man threw the
car into gear and drove straight
into the Potomac River.

♥ ♥ ♥

Don't Be So Touchy

W hen a policeman pulls a car over for speeding he's ready to hear some crazy excuses. But when a Montana Highway Patrol officer pulled over the speeding car of Robert Niel Johnson III, the man didn't try to hide anything. "How come you don't have your pants on?" Officer Darvin Mees asked Johnson. The officer then glanced over at the passenger, Shelby Kauffman, who was a little more discreet. Mees observed that she "somewhat had her pants on." The woman told the officer that she and Johnson had just gotten engaged and started "getting frisky" in the car. Mees asked the man to get out and when he saw the driver stumbling around he arrested him. After only fifteen minutes of deliberation the jury in Johnson's drunk-driving trial threw out the charge, citing lack of evidence. "Anybody caught with his pants down like that would be nervous," the jury's foreman said. And if he hadn't pulled them up, maybe that's why he was stumbling around. ♥

A deaf man in Bennettsville, South Carolina, filed for divorce because his wife "was always nagging him in sign language."

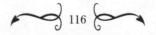

♥ ♥ ♥

Jeffrey Allen Hayes pleaded guilty to strangling Shannon Fay Stevens in West Seattle, Washington, explaining he mistook her for his ex-girlfriend, Barbara Dodge.

♥ ♥ ♥

Who's Better, Who's Better, Who's Best?

An engaged man discovered that his fiancée was seeing another man, and he stormed out of the house to confront him. Stewart Parkes, of Leamington, England, marched down to the local pub to give Clint Gordon, the man who was seeing Parkes's bride-to-be, Christine Browning, a solid thrashing. As the two men argued, Stewart realized that he and Clint had much in common: "We're both builders, we both like football . . . and of course there was Christine," Stewart said. Both men sat down, shared a few pints, and became fast friends—so fast, in fact, that Stewart asked Clint to be best man at his wedding and Clint accepted. "The thought of them getting together and talking about me was awful," said a devastated Christine when she heard the two men were getting on so well. The *News of the World* reported that Stewart and Christine were married in April 2003—side by side with Clint. ♥

In Delaware:

"A person is guilty of aggravated harassment when, in the course of a telephone call, he uses obscene, profane, or vulgar language, or language suggesting that the recipient of the call engage with him or another person in sexual relations of any sort. . . . Aggravated harassment is a misdemeanor."

—Delaware Code Annotated Title 11 § 132 (enacted 1953)

Here Today, Gown Tomorrow

Weddings can be a terribly expensive ordeal, so couples are always trying to find ways to cut costs. Joanne Dixon and Che Dunlop were able to get a greatly discounted rate on the wedding dress—a five-finger discount. They stole the $525 dress from a store in Totnes, south Devon, England, got married, and would have lived happily ever after had it not been for one bad judgment call. In honor of their nuptials, they had their wedding picture, with Joanne decked out in the stolen dress, published in the local newspaper. The shopkeeper, whose dress was stolen, picked up the paper, saw the photo, and called the police. "I was just amazed that she had the cheek to let her picture go in the paper wearing a dress stolen under my very nose," said the shop's proprietor. Joanne Dixon was fined $300 for handling stolen merchandise, and Che was sentenced for stealing the $525 dress. The judge addressed the duress of the dress shop owner and redressed the wedding dress rustlers by giving them a good dressing down. ♥

♥ ♥ ♥

Walter Kern of Long Island
filed for divorce from his wife,
Rana, claiming that she was a
witch and routinely practiced
ritualistic animal sacrifices.

♥ ♥ ♥

The Bride and Gloom

ccording to an article in the April 30, 2003, *Sacramento Bee*, a New Zealand family was struck by a tragedy just two days before their daughter's wedding. The girl's grandfather died, and the bride was sad that he wouldn't be able to see her walk down the aisle. So the family decided that a reasonable solution would be to wheel the deceased grandfather down the aisle first and leave the coffin lid propped open during the wedding ceremony. I wonder if the bride, not knowing whether to wear white for the wedding or black for the funeral, decided on a checkerboard pattern. ♥

After her wedding reception in Crystal River, Florida, Kathy Naylor followed home a guest with whom she had had a fight and was arrested after she reignited the brawl.

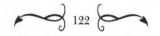

Separate but Equal

wo jailbirds became lovebirds after meeting in prison and falling in love. Victor Thompson was serving time for writing a bad check, and Jennifer Wachenfeld Weiss was in jail for receiving stolen property. They stole each other's hearts and a bond was forged. After they were released from prison, they got married and were immediately charged with violating their probations. As a condition of probation, both had been ordered to stay away from other convicted felons—which included each other. Thompson claimed his probation officer knew about the wedding plans but never mentioned the conflict. I wonder if it was because he wasn't invited to the wedding. ♥

In Georgia:

"A person commits statutory rape when he engages in sexual intercourse with any female under fourteen not his spouse."

—**Georgia Code Annotated §16-6-3 (enacted 1918)**

A Tangled Web

L isa Vanhostauyen, from Dandenong, Australia, spent three months planning her wedding to a man she met in cyberspace. She must have spent all her money on an elaborate computer system because when it came time to buy wedding things, she found herself broke. Since she was already broke, she decided to break the law, too, and she stole a $1,000 wedding dress, a suit for an unnamed man, decorations, ashtrays, wineglasses, and even a stereo to play music during the ceremony. Vanhostauyen pleaded guilty to theft, handling stolen goods, and assaulting the police officer in charge of the investigation. "A lot of people plan weddings in limited financial circumstances and do not resort to stealing," lectured Magistrate Kay Macpherson. For her three months' work planning and stealing for her wedding, the woman was sentenced to a two-month suspended jail term. No word if the mysterious Web-man ever materialized. ♥

The '70s are considered the golden age of sex toys, but the vibrator was created in the '60s—the 1860s. In 1869, Victorian-era doctors used a **steam-powered** unit to treat "female **hysteria**."

—*The History of Sex,* the History Channel, August 1999

Little White Lies

uanita Konold-McIntosh decided to love and cherish her husband even though she didn't have a clue who he really was. During the fraud trial of her "husband" of fifteen years, Eduardo G. McIntosh, Juanita said she was still devoted to him even though he forgot to tell her a few things: (a) Since he still had a valid earlier marriage, Eduardo and Juanita were not legally married; (b) Eduardo was not, nor had he ever been, an Air Force general; (c) the reason he only spent one night a week with her during their entire marriage wasn't because he was on secret intelligence missions—it was because he was spending the other six days with his legitimate family; (d) the reason he stole thousands of dollars from her bank account was to pay the bills for his real family and fund various other schemes and scams; and (e) the reason she didn't hear from him during a four-month period in 1994 wasn't because he was on a top-secret assignment, it was because he was in jail. I bet his real last name wasn't even McIntosh—it was probably Microsoft or Dell. ♥

Another Roadside Attraction

To celebrate Father's Day, Traci Ann Bitz took her husband, Rick Shaver, out to dinner. Since it was his special day, Traci asked him what he was in the mood for, and he said he wanted pasta. But Traci had had pasta the night before, so she wanted different food, and an argument ensued. The argument escalated until Shaver got out of their car in frustration and stormed away. Thinking Shaver might want something hot off the grill, Bitz floored the gas pedal and ran him over. Police noted it was no accident, since they discovered a long patch of burned rubber on the road where she'd peeled out after him. According to police reports, Bitz then spun out in a parking lot, where she stayed to make some phone calls. It was a close shave for Shaver, but he survived the ordeal with only cuts and bruises. While being escorted to the police cruiser in handcuffs, Bitz asked how long she would be detained—she had a massage appointment in less than an hour. Bitz missed her massage (too bad because running someone over can make you tense). She was booked on assault and jailed. It was probably the best Father's Day gift Shaver could ever get. ♥

♥ ♥ ♥

"It was certainly a day to remember. By the end we had a huge pile of toasters stacked up in the corner of the room. We also got two toast holders— it really was very funny," said bride Marion Olphert after receiving thirteen toasters as wedding gifts.

♥ ♥ ♥

I'll Have What They're Having

A couple pleaded no contest to a charge of public indecency for engaging in sex in a booth at a Hardee's restaurant in New Philadelphia, Ohio. During the hearing, the prosecutor told the judge that although this was the couple's first lewdness charge, it was not the first time they had "done something like that." The judge told the couple they should grow up and act their age: The man was seventy and the woman was sixty. ♥

A British woman took another approach to the Lorena Bobbitt strategy. After her boyfriend refused to have sex with her, Amanda Monti ripped off his left testicle with her **bare** hands.

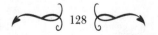

Going in Style

One unfortunate couple, José Agustin Noh and Ana Maria Camara Suarez of Campeche, Mexico, died from carbon monoxide poisoning after having sex in their automobile. In order to cool things down while they heated up, they left the engine running to keep the air-conditioning on. After car-pulating, they fell asleep and eventually succumbed to the carbon monoxide fumes. What makes this story particularly strange is that the car they had sex in and then died in was a hearse. ♥

HIGHEST DIVORCE RATES IN THE WORLD

RANK	COUNTRY	DIVORCES PER 1,000 INHABITANTS PER YEAR
1	Maldives	10.97
2	Belarus	4.63
3	United States	4.34
4	Cuba	3.72
5	Estonia	3.65
6	Panama	3.61
6	Puerto Rico	3.61
8	Ukraine	3.56
9	Russia	3.42
10	Antigua and Barbuda	3.40

Source: United Nations

From SUV to SVU

Bryan Loudermilk of Okeechobee, Florida, died in a most peculiar fashion, and police began an investigation. After questioning the deceased's wife, Stephanie Loudermilk, at length, detectives finally ruled Bryan's death accidental. Apparently, he was a victim of a sexual fetish gone wrong. It was reported that Bryan's body was found in a specially constructed pit, that a board had been placed over him, and that the rear wheel of the couple's sport utility vehicle was parked on top of him. Police believe that Bryan received erotic thrills from being run over. I suppose when his wife told people she still had a crush on her husband, she meant something completely different. ♥

A guest at a wedding in San Antonio, Texas,
apparently brought too many friends along with him.
An argument broke out between the guest and the groom,
and during the wedding reception the groom **shot** him.

It Should Be Called Man-esota

n Minnesota, adultery occurs when a married woman has sexual intercourse with a man other than her husband, whether the man is married or not. Both parties are guilty of a misdemeanor. A prosecution for adultery requires a complaint by a spouse of one of the offenders, unless those spouses are insane. It is a defense to adultery that the man did not know the marital status of the woman. There is no prohibition against sex between a married man and an unmarried woman. ♥

—**Minnesota Statute §609.36 (enacted 1963)**

Following a courtship that lasted several months, one-hundred-year-old Samuel Bukoro married twelve-year-old Nyamihanda in Uganda in 1995.

Two In, Three Out

We've all seen movies where prisoners secretly exchange things through the bars of their cells. But one couple in Britain's Swansea Crown Court building passed something through the bars that you would only see in a different kind of prison movie. An investigation was launched when inmate Donna Stokes became pregnant after having sex with her boyfriend through the bars of their respective holding cells. Both were awaiting a hearing on burglary and theft charges and were in adjoining temporary cells. As Stokes said, "We hadn't seen each other for months." Sounds like a lot more fun than rattling a tin cup against the bars, doesn't it? ♥

DOES SEX MAKE WOMEN SPRINTERS FASTER??

—Reuters headline, August 9, 2002

What's Your Sign?

In our modern society dating is difficult. For a guy, it's hard to know how to approach a woman—should you open the door for her or let her open it herself? Stephen Millhouse of Cedar Rapids, Iowa, was really confused on proper dating etiquette. He was arrested and convicted of burglary after breaking into the apartment of a twenty-one-year-old woman, awakening her, and politely asking for sex—which she declined. When that approach didn't work, Millhouse asked the woman for an actual date. In order to get the man out of her house, the woman gave him her phone number and told him to call her. Not surprisingly, Millhouse did call the woman, she set up a time for them to meet, and he was arrested when he arrived. During the trial, Millhouse's lawyer told the jury his client was too stupid to be dangerous. He then turned to his client sitting in the witness stand and asked, "Did you really think she wanted to see you again?" To which Millhouse exclaimed, "I didn't know for sure. That's why I called." ♥

In Oklahoma:

"It is a felony to seduce and have illicit connection with any unmarried female of previous chaste character under promise of marriage; later marriage is a defense."

—**Oklahoma Statutes Annotated Title 21 §§1120, 1121 (enacted 1910)**

Do You Feel Lucky, Punk? Well, Do You?

After being fired from his job, Stuart Underwood, a police officer in Painesville, Ohio, took his case to arbitration. During the proceedings, arbitrator Dennis Minni sided with Officer Underwood and ruled that "even Clint Eastwood as Dirty Harry took the time to take a last bite from his hot dog before leaving the restaurant to confront the bank robber he saw." I'm sure Freud would question Minni's "hot dog" analogy, as Officer Underwood had been fired for having sex with a woman in his patrol car. Minni noted that "it was his break time, and he [Underwood] testified that he did not shut his radio off. Since he could have received a call for assistance, the time it would take to respond has not been shown to be any greater than it would have been for many other activities." Activities like eating a cream-filled éclair or polishing his nightstick perhaps? Minni ruled in favor of Underwood and ordered he be reinstated with back pay. ♥

♥ ♥ ♥

Shortly after their wedding, Carlos Alarcon-Schroder and his new bride, Marcia Alarcon, were placed in jail. The argument and subsequent arrest started over whose parents they would visit first.

♥ ♥ ♥

A Unique Accompaniment

An overly romantic Italian man wanted to woo his girlfriend by serenading her with love songs. Unfortunately, the man didn't know how to play an instrument, but he knew he could sing if he could just find the right key. He found the right key in the ignition of an empty parked ambulance. So the man stole the ambulance, drove it to his girlfriend's house near Ancona, turned on the siren, and started singing love songs. Well, the neighbors didn't appreciate the singing or the siren and reported the man to the police. "This has to be one of the most bizarre cases we have ever had to deal with," a police spokesman said. "Unfortunately his idea didn't go down well with the neighbors or the hospital, which wanted the ambulance back immediately." ♥

"I meant to kill my wife, but I forgot my glasses."

Said by a sixty-one-year-old retired Army sergeant who shot a woman he mistook for his estranged wife outside a church in Rochester, New York, as reported in the *Seattle Post-Intelligencer*, April 1, 1990

I Wonder Where They're Registered

In June 2003, two Texas prison inmates, Diane Zamora and Steven Mora, received permission to marry even though they've never met and cannot consummate their marriage until, at the earliest, 2036.

Bride-to-be Diane Zamora, a former U.S. Naval Academy midshipman, was sentenced to life in prison for the 1995 murder of a sixteen-year-old girl. The nervous groom, Steven Mora, was serving four years for intimidating a person who had helped put him in prison on an earlier charge. The couple has only exchanged letters and will have to wait a minimum of thirty years before they can share a wedding bed. Because Zamora is in a maximum-security prison, no physical contact can be allowed, according to Texas prison spokesman Larry Fitzgerald. He added that moving Zamora to a lower-security prison wouldn't help, either, since "there are no conjugal visits in Texas prisons."

As a side note, if Diane Zamora takes Steven Mora's last name, she'll be Diane Zamora-Mora. ♥

♥ ♥ ♥

The city to hold the most wedding ceremonies (according to *Guinness World Records 2005: Special 50th Anniversary Edition*) is Las Vegas, Nevada, with over 100 chapels performing approximately 8,400 marriage ceremonies per month—that averages out to about 280 per day or one wedding every 5 minutes, 17 seconds (which is about how long some of the marriages last).

♥ ♥ ♥

Phony Phone Phun

Victor Dragomirescu and his wife, Lucica, were speaking with one another on their cellular phones. Victor claimed to be at his mother's house and Lucica complained about being sick at home. Their conversation went as follows:

LUCICA: "I feel worse than ever. I haven't eaten anything since yesterday and I don't think I can stand it anymore. Thank God we have the mobile phones because I couldn't get out of bed even to answer the other phone. What about you?"

VICTOR: "Oh, don't ask. If you could just see me, I think you wouldn't recognize me. I am all full of dust, as I've been to the mill with some corn. Now I have to gather the fruit in my mother's yard. I can't look at my hands to see how horrible they are."

Neither needed to ask the question "Can you hear me now?" because they both looked up and realized they were standing face-to-face on the beach of Mamaia on the Black Sea, a popular seaside resort. The Ziarul daily reported that the Romanian couple returned home to try and clear up the mess, but said a divorce is likely. Sounds like there was a lot of static between the two even before the fateful phone conversation. ♥

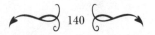

A Clash of Cultures

An Englishman flew all the way to Ladson, South Carolina, to meet and marry a woman with whom he had had a hot Internet romance. When the twenty-seven-year-old arrived, he was surprised to actually meet his future bride, sixty-five-year-old Wynema Faye Shumate. The Englishman was disappointed, to say the least, as Wynema had portrayed herself online as a thirtysomething-year-old. According to police, when the Englishman asked the woman if there was anything else she hadn't told him, she said there was one little thing—she had a carved-up human body in her freezer. It was the corpse of a former housemate who had died of natural causes (I suppose the carving part came in when she tried to get the man's body to fit into the freezer). The woman was charged on two counts of mishandling a dead body but was cleared of any wrongdoing in the man's death. The Englishman decided to cancel the wedding. ♥

In Alabama:

"It is a misdemeanor for a person nineteen or older to engage in sexual contact with a person under sixteen but over twelve."

—**Alabama Code §13A-6-67 (enacted 1977)**

Everyone Got Scrooged

Two days before Christmas 2003, Kim Russell, wife and mother of two, decided to leave her family for another man. She had been carrying on an Internet romance with him, and they agreed to finally meet. She entered the hotel room in Somerset, England, and was so nervous about what she was about to do that she died on the spot. An inquest could find no physical reason for the thirty-year-old woman's death, and in July 2004 ruled it "sudden death syndrome." Merry Christmas, everybody! ♥

In Georgia:

"It is unlawful to be a 'peeping Tom.' A person is guilty of being a 'peeping Tom' if that person peeps through windows or doors on or about the premises of another for the purpose of spying upon or invading the privacy of the persons spied upon."

—Georgia Code Annotated § 16-11-61 (enacted 1919)

All in the Family

In one fell swoop, George Greenhowe of Arbroath, Scotland, shook the family tree from the roots up. The twenty-two-year-old man was living with his wife, Allison; her mother, Pat; and a dozen animals in a small council house. After only ten days of marriage, George divorced Allison. He then announced he had fallen in love with another woman and was going to get married immediately. The woman who stole Allison's place was her mother, Pat. Now George will be his ex-wife's stepfather, and Allison has even agreed to act as her mom's bridesmaid. And you thought stuff like this only happened in West Virginia. ♥

"The fruits hanging by the roots on the lands belonging separately to either the husband or the wife, at the time of the dissolution of the marriage, are equally divided between the husband and the wife."

—Louisiana state divorce law

The Robber Bridegroom

P rospective bride and groom Dorrell Mainer and Kevin Rainey had scheduled a huge extravagant June wedding that included out-of-town guests. The couple planned to pay for their wedding with an expected tax refund, but when the IRS denied the refund, the couple didn't know where to turn. So they turned into bank robbers. Three days before their wedding, the duo walked down the aisle of a Chase Manhattan bank in Brooklyn and announced a holdup. The teller delayed getting them the money, and the criminal couple was arrested and charged with attempted robbery. They admitted they didn't know how to pay the caterer and didn't want to disappoint their out-of-town guests, who will now have to visit them in prison. The nearly-wed's food will soon be catered by the state. ♥

Chop-Steaks and Chopsticks

Seventy-year-old Mattie Charlene Dyer married seventy-one-year-old Yang Yukun, in Calgary, Alberta, and they settled down together there as husband and wife. Mattie is an American-born teacher who speaks only English and the groom is a retired pipe fitter from Beijing who speaks only Chinese. Mattie said, in English, their marriage is "hard to explain. [But there is] an electricity [and] a magnetism between us." Yang apparently didn't have anything to add; or he did, but just knew she wouldn't understand him. ♥

♥ ♥ ♥

Bringing a different twist to the "Mile High Club," a high-flying couple tied the knot on a wing and a prayer when they took their wedding vows strapped to the wings of three 1940s biplanes. Caroline Hackwood, Justin Bunn, and Methodist minister the Reverend George Brigham, each on a different plane, conducted the ceremony using microphones to communicate with guests on the ground.

♥ ♥ ♥

A Story That's Hard to Swallow

A newlywed couple from Massachusetts, Mark and Hillary Meltz, were finally able to relax and enjoy their Hawaiian honeymoon safe in the knowledge that their wedding ring had been "returned." Mark left the wedding ring on a counter, and when he returned to retrieve it, it was gone. He checked with Hillary and his brother, but no one knew where the ring was. It was soon discovered that the couple's Labrador retriever, Liza, had retrieved it, and an X ray confirmed the new location of the ring. On the day of their wedding, Mark had presented Hillary with an X ray of the dog's stomach that showed the unmistakable image of the ring. Fortunately, she'd laughed instead of cried, and they were pronounced man and wife. Mark's parents told the couple to go on their honeymoon, and they would watch the dog—at both ends. After the parents loaded the dog up with treats, Liza finally vomited and the ring came clinking out. I suppose this makes the ring a little more bearable to wear than if it had exited at the other end. ♥

♥ ♥ ♥

In June 2004, the United States Court of Appeals for the 11th Circuit upheld an Alabama ban on the sale of sex toys. The court of appeals decided by a 2–1 vote to uphold the 1998 law, struck down twice by a lower court. If convicted Alabamians can now get up to a year of jail time and up to $10,000 in fines.

♥ ♥ ♥

Hey, Uncle Ben Is Here, Too

The tradition of throwing rice as the bride and groom exit the church took a bad turn for one Italian bride. Paola Bonsangue ran through the gauntlet of rice throwers after her wedding in Lecco, Italy, and one grain lodged in her inner ear. Her groom, Burno Ratti, and several family members tried in vain to remove the grain, but it had worked its way too far in. Paola was rushed to the hospital where doctors successfully removed the grain of rice and congratulated her on her wedding. The wedding reception was delayed as guests converted the rice-riddled area into a waiting room and stayed until the bride returned from the emergency room. No word on injuries suffered from the throwing of the bouquet. ♥

A woman from Berlin, Germany, Heidi Berger, filed for divorce from her husband of sixty-nine years. In divorce papers she listed the cause of the divorce as "**lack of sex**." Heidi was one hundred and Hans, her husband, was one hundred and one.

Tongue in Cheek

he traditional kiss at the end of the wedding ceremony is a memorable event in the life of any woman. But for Vivian Frazier, her wedding kiss is the last one she's going to get from her new husband for at least two years. Authorities say Frazier, who married Jeremy Guinther in an Indiana jailhouse, slipped him more than a little tongue—she added two grams of methamphetamine. A Vigo County jail guard became suspicious after seeing Guinther with a slight bulge in his cheek immediately following the kiss. According to a sheriff's department report, when authorities ordered him to open his mouth, Guinther swallowed. Frazier was sentenced to two years in prison for felony trafficking with an inmate. Guinther pleaded guilty to felony drug possession and unrelated charges of theft and drug possession. After this incident, the warden enacted a new rule against kissing during jailhouse weddings. Now if he could only stop all the other kissing that goes on in the prison. ♥

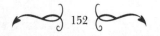

Stop Pointing Your Finger

The aptly named David Battle of Victorville, California, suffered a mangled left hand and severe wounds to his legs in a firefight in Fallujah. A nineteen-year-old lance corporal in the Marines, Battle overheard his doctors discussing cutting off his wedding ring in order to save as much of his finger as possible. But in a Leonardo DiCaprio gesture, Battle told doctors to cut off his finger and save the ring—as a reminder of his love for his wife, Devon. In a bittersweet moment, the doctors amputated Battle's finger and removed the ring intact. But in the pandemonium that followed they somehow lost the ring. I'm sure Battle gave them the finger, too. ♥

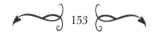

"The United States has the lowest percentage among Western nations of children who grow up with both biological parents: 63 percent."

—*The State of Our Unions 2005*, the annual report by the National Marriage Project at New Jersey's Rutgers University

Mrs. Taken Identity

oseph Pileggi filed a lawsuit in Akron, Ohio, seeking financial damages over his accidental 1997 marriage to Carli Buchanan. Pileggi claimed he didn't mean to marry Buchanan; he thought he was marrying his longtime girlfriend, Ducile Palermo, who is Buchanan's mother. In the suit, Pileggi claimed he did not realize until two years after the marriage that the "wrong" woman's name was on the marriage license. Buchanan is countering Pileggi's claim, stating that the man knew what he had done and that he had even consummated the marriage with her on the wedding night. This is a case of "like mother like daughter," except the man liked the daughter and wanted to marry the mother. ♥

haron Tarr and Robbie Layne, both serving
a life sentence for murder in England's
Broadmoor Prison, called off their wedding
after reading a newspaper article about their evil pasts.
Tarr was labeled the Devil's Daughter during her trial
for the brutal stabbing murder of eighteen-year-old Katie
Rackliff when Tarr was twelve. The groom-to-be had
beaten and stabbed his mother to death and then gouged
her eyes out because he thought she was giving his sister
more attention. "Obviously they didn't tell each other
about their pasts," said a nurse at the Berkshire top
security hospital, where they met.

Flocking Together

ccording to an article in the April 1, 2001, edition of the *Albuquerque Journal,* fifteen-year-old Sierra Kirkpatrick married forty-eight-year-old Mr. Sauren Crow in Las Vegas. Nevada state law requires a minor's parent to grant permission before the ceremony becomes official, and Sierra's mom did just that. When Sierra's father (the mother's ex-husband) found out about the marriage, he went ballistic. Sierra's mother and others tried to calm down the flustered father by saying the couple was perfect for each other; they were both artsy types, dressed in the "Goth" look, and actually looked a little alike (especially with their all-black clothes and long black hair). In a few years I'm sure Sierra will see things a little differently when her husband's long black hair starts falling out and his "Goth" look becomes the middle-aged "Sloth" look. ♥

"It is unlawful for any male person within the corporate limits of the city of Ottumwa to wink at any female person with whom he is unacquainted."

—Municipal code of Ottumwa, Iowa

Money-Back Guarantee

orge Giovanni Bravo Morales of Medellin, Colombia, had a fight with his wife and stormed out of his house in January 2004. His wife became concerned when he didn't return for several days, and nearly a week after his disappearance, she received a ransom letter demanding more than $1,200 for his return. Radio Cadena Nacional reported that the woman quickly turned the matter over to the police, who started an investigation. It didn't take them long to track down the man's kidnapper because it turned out that Mr. Morales had kidnapped himself. He told police the reason for his self-napping was "I wanted to know if she still cared for me. I've always loved her, but things were bad, and I wanted her to notice me. I beg for her forgiveness." Mr. Morales was charged with extortion. I can almost guarantee that if he wanted to know how his wife felt about him, he got an earful when he got home. ♥

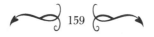

Waxing Romantic

Nominating himself for the "Most Romantic Night of Your Life" award, one love-struck German laid out hundreds of candles in the shape of a heart anticipating his girlfriend's arrival. The candles spelled out the words "You set my heart on fire," but unfortunately they did more than that—they set his whole house on fire. Firefighters arrived instead of his girlfriend and battled the blaze for more than an hour before getting it under control. No one was hurt, but authorities estimated that damage to the house was about $50,000. Next time I suggest he try rose petals. ♥

HIGHEST TEENAGE PREGNANCY RATES
IN DEVELOPED COUNTRIES

RANK	COUNTRY	PREGNANCIES PER 1,000
1	Russia	101.7
2	United States	83.6
3	Bulgaria	83.3
4	United Kingdom (England and Wales)	46.9
5	Australia	43.7
6	Sweden	24.9
7	Netherlands	12.2

Source: BBC, 2004

It's Over

A couple parked on a hillside west of Lujan de Cuyo, Argentina, became passionate and soon things really got rocking. In fact, their car rolled over the cliff and plummeted some three hundred yards into a ravine. After they fell for each other, the couple pulled themselves from the wreckage with no serious injuries. ♥

♥ ♥ ♥

Minne Herv, a forty-two-year-old Belgian man, got to live out his lifelong fantasy when he married his former elementary school teacher. Herv had a crush on Daniella Waltens when he was six and she was eighteen. Decades later, the two met again; Herv "got the same goose bumps as I did when I was six," but Waltens didn't feel the same way about him. A romantic getaway to the south of France not only got Herv some extra credit, it also got him Waltens's hand in marriage.

♥ ♥ ♥

A Very Weak Link

n April 2001, a man in a Vancouver, Washington, courtroom professed his love to a woman he had dated briefly twenty-five years earlier. During his trial, John K. Flora served as his own council and questioned the woman whom he was charged with stalking. Flora badgered the woman trying to make her admit she was in love with him, a fact she consistently denied. The woman became more horrified and hostile after every question and Flora, mistaking her rage for passion, pulled out a $5,000 engagement ring and screamed, "Marry me! You mean everything to me! Please!" The woman was terrified at Flora's actions, as was the judge, who ordered deputies to chain the man to his chair. ♥

The Trial of Jack Sprat

atthew Long was accused of assaulting his girlfriend, Vicki Smith, and was on trial in a Cincinnati courtroom in September 2003. Smith had Long arrested on claims that he choked her with a dog's leash and beat her. The leash, however, couldn't be introduced as evidence, as the dog had reportedly eaten it. Long testified that what really happened was that he grabbed Smith to prevent her from walking out on him, and she dragged him through the house. Seeing the evidence in front of him, along with the accused and the victim, the judge ruled Long was innocent of the charges. The large and small of the matter was that Long weighed 116 pounds and had only one leg while his girlfriend, Smith, weighed 250 pounds and admitted she could throw Long around "like a rag doll." ♥

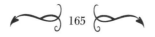

♥ ♥ ♥

A woman in Sweden was arrested for domestic assault after she fractured her husband's jaw and skull because he refused to go on a march in Stockholm. The march was to protest domestic violence.

♥ ♥ ♥

A Lot Slower Than Dial-Up

Getting tangled up in a new romance on the Web is becoming more and more common. One man, Charles Gonsoulin, met a woman on the Internet and even though she lived in Canada, he felt compelled to meet her. There was only one problem. Due to a 1984 robbery conviction, Gonsoulin was barred from entering Canada. Gonsoulin said, "But I was a desperate man." He decided he would sneak across the border from Pembina, North Dakota, and visit his Canadian girlfriend in Winnipeg. The February walk "was a lot worse than I thought," Gonsoulin said, because the ground was covered in heavy snow. "When I found him, he was babbling and incoherent," said Corporal Don McKenna of the Royal Canadian Mounted Police. "He didn't know who he was or where he was." So did he ever hyperlink up with his cybermate? Nope. In fact, after walking more than one hundred hours in the snow, Gonsoulin had only traveled a little over four miles. He was treated in a hospital and then deported back to the United States—well, most of him was deported. The exchange rate for his trip was pretty severe. He lost five toes and all of his fingers due to frostbite. "I will never regret it. I'm in love," Gonsoulin said. He can still surf the Net, but his bowling days are over. ♥

In California:

"Any person who participates in an act of sodomy with any person of any age while confined in any state prison, as defined in Section 4504, or in any local detention facility, as defined in Section 6031.4, shall be punished by imprisonment in the state prison or in a county jail for not more than one year."

—California State Penal Code § 286/2005

To Everything, Turn, Turn, Turn

A couple from Brnicko, Czechoslovakia, were enjoying a roll in the hay when it suddenly became a roll and a "Hey!" While sowing some wild oats in a field, they heard the terrifying sound of a farmer on a tractor taking a shortcut through his land. The farmer did more than just take a shortcut—he also cut the couple up fairly well, causing severe injuries to the woman's chest and the man's buttocks. The nearly cropped couple tried to keep the accident a secret, since they were embarrassed and unmarried, but doctors and insurers tracked down the origin of their injuries. That's what happens in a relationship when there's an attractee and a-tractor. ♥

John Turner of Thornaby-on-Tees, England, sought and was granted a divorce from his wife, Pauline, on the grounds of **unreasonable behavior**. The British man couldn't stand his wife's compulsive habit of **rearranging the furniture** every day of their thirty-eight-year marriage.

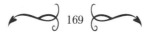

When You Care Enough to Send the Very Best

There seems to be a greeting card for just about anybody or anything these days, but Cathy Gallagher of Bethesda, Maryland, has found a hallmark of a niche: married people having affairs. Gallagher, who is married and claims to have never had an affair, defends her cheating, uh, greeting, cards because: "People who are involved in affairs are not bad people. A lot of people meet the right person at the wrong time." So why would a faithful woman become involved in such an affair? "You don't have to be a murderer to write a murder mystery," she said. ♥

Joe Kern, a maintenance worker in Tennessee, was using a nail gun when he slipped and fired a one-inch spike into his breastbone, piercing his heart. But Kern refused to go directly to the emergency room because he wanted to stop by his house and reassure his wife that he was all right. He was later airlifted to Vanderbilt Hospital in Nashville, where surgeons removed the nail and repaired his punctured right ventricle.

Sanitation Relation

Unfortunately, a lot of marriages end up in the trash, but one London couple started their union in the trash—or at least the garbage truck. Sonia Chamberlain arrived at her wedding in her fiancé's garbage truck, which was decked out in ribbons and balloons. Chamberlain said she did this to memorialize the fact that when she first laid eyes on husband-to-be Guy Whetton, he was backing up his garbage truck near her house. Whetton knew Chamberlain's love for him wasn't a bunch of rubbish because "if she could fancy me at the wheel of a dustcart, I knew she must be serious, and we just went on from there." Now Whetton is Chamberlain's refuse from the storm. ♥

In Maryland:

"Adultery is a misdemeanor, punishable by a $10 fine."

—Annotated Code of Maryland Article 27 §3 (enacted 1749)

Dog-Day Afternoon

he term "gay bashing" has sadly become part of our national lexicon. But a Florida man, George Finley, took this term to bizarre heights when he bashed his wife's dog to death because he thought it was gay. Sheriff Mike McQuaig said Finley "felt that the dog was a queer-type dog and it made him angry." Witnesses reported that the fifty-eight-year-old man became furious when the neutered Yorkshire terrier kept trying to mount the family's male Jack Russell terrier. Finley was accused of hitting the dog with a vacuum cleaner wand and causing the little animal to lapse into a coma after heaving it against a tree. Finley maintains that the dog's death was accidental. ♥

Clean Up on Aisle Three

Frode Jonassen didn't pay much attention when his girlfriend, Tone Soerensen, stepped into the back room at a Norwegian grocery store, because she worked there. But he heard over the PA system, "I love you and want to marry you. You have ten seconds to decide." For Frode, this was a bigger decision than paper or plastic. When the customers started counting aloud the remaining seconds, he nearly panicked, reported *Verdens Gang* on February 9, 2000. At the last second he yelled out, "Yes!" and soon he and Tone went from walking down a grocery aisle to walking down a church aisle. ♥

Kire Iliovski from Prilep in Macedonia talked on the phone for more than 135 hours to an extremely friendly and provocative woman he thought could be his **perfect** future bride. When he received a phone bill for **$15,322**, he realized he hadn't been having a conversation with a woman arranged by a marriage agency, but in fact he'd been speaking to a woman from a **phone sex** line.

♥ ♥ ♥

According to the *St. Petersburg Times,* city officials in Arcadia, Florida, voted to force Beverly Georges to exhume the body of her husband, Rick, from their backyard. Rick had requested the grave site, a violation of city zoning rules, so he could be united with his beloved pit bull, Bocephus.

♥ ♥ ♥

Dumber Than a Box of Rocks

Great things come in small packages, but you've just got to make sure the right package gets to the right person.

According to news reports, Mircea Rau bought two necklaces—one for his wife and one for his mistress, each bearing the relevant woman's engraved initials. He could tell the two women apart, and he could tell the two necklaces apart, but apparently he couldn't tell the two packages apart. He accidentally (are there any real accidents?) gave his wife the wrong necklace, and she threw a fit. She also threw an ashtray that knocked Rau unconscious. He was taken to the hospital and his wife has gone to court seeking a divorce. No word on what happened when the girlfriend opened her gift. ♥

STATE: SEX WITH MINOR WORTH FELONY CHARGE

—El Paso (Texas) *Times,* July 11, 2001

Bought for a Song

German pop singer Christian Anders figured out how to finance his liver transplant. The singer made a deal with millionaire Michael Liecher to "loan out" Anders's girlfriend for a year. Twenty-year-old Jenna Kartes was offered to Liecher in exchange for 500,000 DM so Anders could get a much-needed liver transplant. The bartered babe said, "I was shocked myself when I heard about this offer. Christian and Michael decided on it behind my back." But this slave to love didn't seem too angry about being put on the auction block. "I will sleep with Michael because I love Christian," Kartes said. "Perhaps he can then afford a new liver. Why should I feel like a prostitute about it?" ♥

A woman in Canon City, Colorado, divorced her husband because he forced her to "duck under the **dashboard** whenever they drove past his **girlfriend's** house."

♥ ♥ ♥

Jeannie M. Patrinos was
sentenced to five years' probation
for sexual assault. Patrinos, who
was estranged from her husband,
broke into his home, climbed
into bed with him, and was
caught "having sex" with him
against his will by the man's
girlfriend, who was sleeping
beside him in the same bed
at the time.

♥ ♥ ♥

Still Crazy After All These Years

aul Simon had a number one hit in 1976 called "Fifty Ways to Leave Your Lover," but I'm sure even the master lyricist never thought of leaving the way one Houston, Texas, man did. Marvin Latryl Smith was having an argument with his girlfriend and thought he would scare her by parking his car on a set of railroad tracks. Well, the girlfriend jumped out of the car and made some tracks of her own, and Smith quickly followed. When Smith heard a train whistle, he didn't just slip out the back, Jack, or make a new plan, Stan, he just ran back and jumped into his car (he didn't even drop off the key, Lee, and he certainly didn't set himself free). The *Houston Chronicle* reported that Smith's stunt made quite an impact on his girlfriend, but not nearly as big as the one it made on Smith. Smith found the fifty-first way to leave his lover, but in doing so he left his life in pieces. ♥

As a student at Arizona State in 1999, Arizona Cardinals running back J. R. Redmond was tricked into marriage by an athletic department employee. Redmond owed the woman a few hundred dollars for phone bills and a trip to Vegas, but when he tried to repay her, she refused. She claimed that what he had done was in violation of NCAA rules and the only way he would be able to get away with taking the monetary gifts was to marry her. He did.

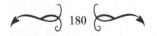

Movers and Shakers

orrine Galford of Marlow, New Hampshire, moved back in with her husband in April 2003 to give their love another chance and maybe to give herself another chance, too. A year before their reunion, Galford pleaded innocent of trying to poison her husband, and while awaiting trial, she decided she should move back in with him. Several months later, Galford accused her husband of raping and beating her, and he retaliated by filing for divorce, claiming Galford was trying to retain possession of the house for herself. Shortly before the judge ruled they could move in together again, Galford's lawyer was quoted as saying the two "are not denying there have been some substantial problems [with the marriage]." ♥

A Romanian bridegroom ended up in the hospital suffering from multiple injuries to the head and chest after overzealous guests threw him in the air but failed to catch him.

My Money's in the Other Vault

n ad in the June 9, 2005, edition of the *Columbus Dispatch* read: "Marriage Died Before Husband Did" and offered an unused coffin for sale. Dixie Fisher and soon-to-be divorced, not dead, husband, David Budd, purchased the steel casket from a friend who works at a metal salvage business. Too bad he couldn't salvage their marriage. Fisher planned to have her remains cremated but bought the casket for Budd thinking it would be a good investment for the future. But the future was now, and Fisher had to pay legal fees for the divorce. She hoped the coffin would cough up some cash and was asking $980. If Fisher's accountant ever asks if she has any buried assets, she's going to have some explaining to do. ♥

William Joseph Wolfe, a hospital nurse from Henderson, Texas, drew a bath for his wife complete with bubbles and romantic candles, but he also tried to throw in something else—a radio. The woman caught the radio before it hit the water and, suspecting he was up to something, checked his computer and discovered he had visited Web sites dealing with bathtub electrocutions just days before. A hospital spokeswoman said, and I'm not making this up, that she was "shocked at what has happened."

Jumpin' Jack Flash

One man's expression of love for his girlfriend made a big splash. A thirty-eight-year-old Oregon man, Todd Grannis, climbed up a ten-foot scaffold as girlfriend, Melissa Kuseik, and about a hundred other people watched. Once at the top Grannis set himself on fire and then jumped into a swimming pool to extinguish the flames. He leaped out of the water, dropped on one knee in front of Kuseik, and popped the question. "Honey, you make me hot. I hope I'm getting the point across that I'm on fire for you." Kuseik accepted his July 2005 plummeting pyrotechnic proposal but let him know that she was hot under the collar that he had put himself in such danger. ♥

An Orlando, Florida, man was allegedly shot to death by his wife following a fight over their satellite-TV controls.

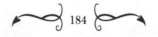

♥ ♥ ♥

In order to save his marriage
from divorce, a Hong Kong man
was forced to file a lawsuit
against a teenage girl to make her
admit that the romantic text
message she sent to his mobile
phone was done so by mistake.

♥ ♥ ♥

Enter at Your Own Risk

fter their November 2003 wedding, newlyweds Jackie and Karl Fekete retired to their bridal suite in a North Wales hotel. The couple was relaxing au naturel in the glow of their love when another hotel guest opened their door and claimed the room was his. Jackie said, "Karl leaped up red-faced and stark naked" to confront the other man. The argument quickly escalated to a fistfight, and Jackie stepped in as peacemaker. The two men wrestled with each other, and Jackie suddenly found herself forced out into the hallway, locked out of her hotel room, and to top it all off she was naked. When she finally made it back into the room, Karl was nowhere to be found and, she said, "I spent our wedding night alone." Karl was arrested for resisting arrest and spent his wedding night in jail after someone from the hotel reported the disturbance. Jackie decided that she and her four children wouldn't feel safe around Karl and his hot temper, so she dumped him the following day. The man who had entered their room, started the fight, and ended Karl's marriage had made a mistake—Karl and Jackie were in the right room all along. ♥

STUDENT EXCITED DAD GOT HEAD JOB

—*University Daily Kansan,* April 24, 2002
Father of Kansas State University student gets head coaching job.

A Painful Strip Show

E dward Marriot told a jury at Derby Crown Court in Derbyshire, England, in June 2004 that Elaine Martinez, his girlfriend, has "the nicest personality you can get" when she's in a good mood. But apparently when she's in a bad mood, you'd better watch out. Early in 2004, the forty-eight-year-old former bricklayer's girlfriend accused him of injecting her with an unknown substance and seeing another woman. This had put her in one of her "bad" moods. She reportedly whipped Edward with a belt, ordered him to drop his pants, and poured paint stripper on his genitals. She then accused him of bugging her mobile phone and threw more paint stripper on him. She called an ambulance, for herself, because she was feeling ill as a reaction to the mystery substance he had allegedly injected into her. But it was Marriot who was admitted to the hospital because while he was at his girlfriend's bedside, he and the nurse noticed his genitals were bleeding. During Martinez's trial, Marriot told the court he didn't fight back because "you can't hit a woman." Besides, Martinez is bigger than he is. Marriot admitted that Martinez had assaulted him before, but that he never reported it because he didn't want her to get into trouble. ♥

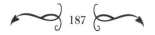

♥ ♥ ♥

The Hudood Ordinance
is a law in Pakistan, enacted in
1979 under the Zia-ul-Haq's
Islamization process, which
criminalizes all extramarital sex,
including adultery or fornication.
Under the Hudood Ordinance,
a woman must have four pious
male Muslim witnesses to
prove rape. The punishment
for adultery is stoning to death
for married couples and 100
lashes for unmarried persons.

♥ ♥ ♥

A Gut Feeling

atrina Grant was having cold feet about her upcoming wedding, so her fiancé, Luke, did something to take her mind off it. He stabbed her. The thirty-six-year-old Warwickshire woman received twelve stitches and was treated for a collapsed lung after the attack. But her lung was the only thing that collapsed—her love for Luke didn't. In June 2004, a month after hearing the sound of an ambulance siren, she heard wedding bells when she and her groom walked down the aisle. I'm sure the guests were nervous and concerned about the marriage, especially when the bride and groom cut the cake. Katrina said, "[People] don't understand how I could marry Luke after what he did, but no one knows him like I do." But I'll bet the guests knew better than to give the couple cutlery as a wedding gift. ♥

♥ ♥ ♥

A mourner at a funeral procession in County Galati, Romania, was surprised to see a naked Orthodox priest and a naked woman forcibly expelled from a house and land in the middle of the death march. The priest had married the young woman to her husband three weeks earlier, and the couple was caught by her husband doing more than speaking in tongues.

♥ ♥ ♥

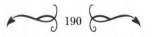

A Limo for Lame-O

ayne Gethers was "enjoying the company of an unidentified female" in the backseat of his limousine in August 2004 when another limo approached. The other limo was driven by his wife, Yvesnane, and their four children were along for the ride. When Yvesnane saw her husband with another woman, she smashed her car into his—several times. Wayne peeled out, but Yvesnane tailed him, continuing to slam into him in a chase that reached fifty mph. Wayne explained that he and Yvesnane had been trying to work through some marital problems, and he was driven into the arms of another woman because of an argument with his wife about the way she dresses. Perhaps this limo driver was stretching the truth a little. ♥

Mr. and Mrs. Worsham sued the United States because the wife voluntarily had an affair with a drug rehab counselor.

—*Worsham v. United States,* 828 F.2d 1515 (11th Circuit, 1987)

The Gift That Keeps on Giving

An unidentified woman from Virginia Beach, Virginia, sued her former lover for knowingly and intentionally giving her genital herpes. In documents filed in September 2004, the woman sought $5 million in compensatory damages and $350,000 in punitive damages, claiming the man persuaded her several times to engage in unprotected sex and "intentionally withheld the fact that he was infected." Her lawsuit further stated the man lied because he claimed to have tested negative for sexually transmitted diseases. The man's attorney, Brian Kantor, countered the woman's accusations because Virginia law makes it illegal to sue someone while engaging in a criminal act yourself. The crime she was committing while the man gave her herpes—sexual intercourse outside marriage. Basically, the woman fell victim to legal claptrap. ♥

Japanese police have charged an unnamed Osaka man with attempting to obtain a divorce by using a **stand-in wife** in court. In June 2004, the man's real wife found out about the divorce and asked the court to **nullify** it.

A Slight Trailer Hitch

railer-home resident Leroy Brown of Pine Bluff, Arkansas, accused his wife of having an affair. He grabbed the pair of pants he claimed she wore during the extramarital activity and set them on fire. Brown was consumed in anger, but he dropped the torched trousers after they burned his fingers, and the mobile home quickly became consumed in flames. Brown was held on arson charges in September 2004 while prosecutors reviewed the case. Well, at least he had a place to sleep. ♥

Jeremiah Frank Dubois pleaded guilty to rape in August 2002 in Raleigh, North Carolina. He explained that he committed the crime so he could have **one last fling** before his wedding.

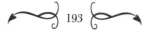

He Said, She Said

In the year 2000, Canadian Susan Macintosh moved in with her then-common-law husband, Ray Lindley. Soon the couple celebrated the birth of their first child and seemed to be the perfect little family. But bad news struck their household in January 2003 when Ray told Susan he had cancer and needed to go to Montreal for treatment. That's when things changed for the worse. Ray did get treatment but not for cancer, which he didn't have. What he did have, he had removed—Ray had a sex-change operation. When Cara-Anne, Ray's new identity, returned, Susan was aghast at seeing his feminine side and decided to sever their relationship. In mid-2004, Ray/Cara-Anne visited, and possibly having forgotten to take his hormone pills, became enraged and struck her twenty times with a tire iron. Susan survived the attack but required major reconstructive surgery, not as reconstructive as Ray/Cara-Anne's, however. Ray/Cara-Anne was sentenced to five years for the assault but reports never revealed whether he went to a man's prison or she went to a woman's prison. ♥

Sedan If You Do, Sedan If You Don't

heresa M. Wilson of Curtis, Washington, caught her ex-boyfriend with another woman and vowed revenge for the betrayal. The opportunity for retribution came in November 2004 when Theresa saw her boyfriend on the road and rammed his car three times. The driver wisely stayed in his car until the police arrived and when he emerged from the damaged 1987 Chevrolet Sprint, Theresa yelled out, "Oh my God, oh my God, that's not my boyfriend." She was right; it wasn't her boyfriend. It wasn't his car, either, as he drove a 1988 Chevrolet Spectrum. The driver, who was innocently heading to work at the time of the misplaced malevolence, said, "Things like that just don't happen around here." Theresa was charged with second-degree assault and should have been forced to take an automobile identification course. ♥

"Every citizen has the right to shoot to kill if necessary when escorting a woman home from a quilting party and another man interferes and threatens to shoot him."

—**Mississippi common law**

What's Behind Door Number One?

Police spokesman Don Aaron of Nashville, Tennessee, said, "From time to time, you come across a case with very unique—even bizarre—circumstances." The case he was referring to revolved around Martha Freeman; her husband, Jeffrey; her lover, Rafael DeJesus Rocha-Perez; and a closet. It's not about her husband, Jeffrey, coming out of the closet; it's about Rafael coming out of the Freemans' closet after living in it for over a month. Apparently Martha allowed her lover, Rafael, to live in the family closet without Jeffrey knowing about it. One night in April 2005, Jeffrey heard snoring coming from the closet. He told Martha that he was going for a walk, and that he wanted the source of the snoring out of the house by the time he got back. When Jeffrey returned, Rafael was out of the closet, and his temper was out of control. The closet drama reached its crescendo when Rafael forced Jeffrey into the bathroom and bludgeoned him to death. I guess Rafael just became unhinged after living behind the closet door for so long. ♥

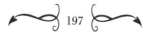

Charles Grubbs and Melody Wyman planned to marry at "the most beautiful cathedral in the world"—the summit of Mount Rainier. During the ceremony a strong gale blew the couple and the minister into a crevasse—all three were rescued by helicopter.

Accuse Me! Excuse Me?

The *People's Daily* reported in April 2005 that thirty-nine-year-old She Xianglin of Shayang County in China's Hubei Province had served eleven years in prison when some new evidence appeared. Xianglin was implicated when his wife, Zhang, disappeared in 1994, and when police later found a badly decomposed female corpse, he was arrested on suspicion of murder. Xianglin, who was a part-time police patrol officer, said, "At first, I insisted I was not the murderer. But later I could not bear the endless interrogation, and I said I did it." The admitted killer was sentenced to death, but his sentence was later reduced to fifteen years' imprisonment, which was one of the luckiest things that ever happened to him. The other lucky thing occurred when his wife, Zhang, happened by to visit relatives in the area. Zhang, who had obviously not been killed by Xianglin and arrived in town with a new husband and son, stated, "I really didn't know what had happened to [Xianglin], and I thought he would live a better life after I left." Xianglin promised to sue the government for compensation for his wrongful imprisonment and emotional trauma. So the government is going to pay for its mistake: not the mistake of imprisoning the wrong man but the costly mistake of reducing his sentence instead of going ahead with the execution. ♥

PIG NOT DEGRADED BY TELEVISED SEXUAL EXPERIENCE, BRITISH WATCHDOG RULES

—Agence France-Presse headline, November 29, 2004

One from Column A and One from Column B

S ome men have a fantasy about being with two women at the same time, and one Kenyan man actually had that fantasy come true. But Peter Amalembiye of Mumias, Kenya, didn't fantasize about two women showing up before his wedding ceremony—both dressed as brides. When Peter arrived at the church, he saw two groups of people each surrounding a woman decked out in a wedding dress. One was the woman to whom he had proposed marriage, Lilian Anyango, and the other was his former girlfriend, Esther Atieno. Esther's supporters raised objections during the ceremony, with one man shouting at Peter, "Either Amalembiye marries Atieno or there will be no wedding." Instead of rice, Peter threw a fit and hit the man with a chair. A fight broke out, and the police were called in to control the situation. In Peter's case, more was certainly not better. ♥

In New Mexico:

"It is unlawful for persons who are not married to one another to cohabit as husband and wife. Upon the first conviction, the offenders will only be warned by the judge to cease and desist the unlawful cohabitation. It is a misdemeanor to persist in committing the crime after being warned."

—New Mexico Statutes Annotated §30-10-2 (enacted 1953)

Don't Turn the Other Cheek

It's funny how two people can see the same incident and remember the events differently. That was the case in the stabbing of Warren Frendell by his live-in girlfriend, Gail Bergman. Detective Aaron Ring of the Fairbanks, Alaska, police department quoted Frendell as saying that he and Bergman were drinking, they had an argument, and she stabbed him in the buttocks with two knives. Bergman remembers the story a little differently. She claims that Frendell showed up at her door naked with the knives already sticking out of his gluteus. Police questioned Bergman's story and pointed out that the knives matched the cutlery set in her kitchen. "I've been asking him where those knives were for the last three weeks," she said. We've all heard the expression "She's a real pain in the butt," but for Frendell that phrase couldn't have been truer. ♥

A man in Tarittville, Connecticut, filed for divorce because his wife left him a note on the refrigerator that read: "I won't be home when you return from work. Have gone to the bridge club. There'll be a recipe for your dinner at seven o'clock on Channel Two."

All the News That's Fit to Print

Shortly after Leo D. Youngblood of Muncie, Indiana, received a marriage license, he received a warrant for his arrest. Leo's wife, Michelle, was casually reading the listing of issued marriage licenses in the newspaper when she came across a name she recognized, and one she didn't. The one she recognized was her husband, Leo, and the one she didn't recognize was Leo's new wife, Rebecca J. Copley. She reported the second marriage to the police in July 2002, and Leo was arrested on bigamy charges. ♥

♥ ♥ ♥

Tina Rae Beavers of Great Falls, Montana, energetically complied with her jailed husband's request that she strip naked and writhe around on the ground separating the city's jail and the courthouse so he could watch from his cell window. The man enjoyed seeing Beavers in action but wasn't able to warn her when police arrived and arrested her.

♥ ♥ ♥

A Ticket to Ride

In August 2002, Deputy D. M. Stout Jr. of Stafford County, Virginia, was on night patrol when he observed a car with an out-of-state license plate parked suspiciously at a shopping center. The *Free Lance-Star* reported that Deputy Stout ran a computer check on the plate, which revealed the car had been stolen in Maryland. When car thief Homas William Cauffman was confronted by the deputy, he explained he just wanted to visit his girlfriend, who was locked up in the Rappahannock Regional Jail, and in order to get there, he needed a car. A simple explanation from an obviously simple-minded man. ♥

❤ ❤ ❤

In 1872, morality crusader Anthony Comstock (1844–1915) drafted an antiobscenity bill, strong-armed his way into Congress, and amazingly got them to turn the bill into a new law. On March 3, 1873, Congress created the Comstock Act, which defined contraceptives as obscene and illicit and made it a federal offense to disseminate birth control through the mail or across state lines.

❤ ❤ ❤

A Word of Warning

Jorge Armando Flores was making love to his girlfriend when she whispered in his ear, "In order to fulfill one of my sexual fantasies [I need you to close your eyes]." The *El Comercio* Web site reported that when Flores complied, the woman grabbed a knife from his trousers and stabbed him in the neck and chest. She then called the police to confess what she had done and to have Flores taken to the hospital. Police reported in September 2002 that the Monterrey, Mexico, woman stabbed her boyfriend because he continually called out the name Veronica when they made love. Veronica was the name of Flores's ex-girlfriend. "Sticks and stones may break my bones, but names can never hurt me"—true, but only if you're sure you say the right name. ♥

SEX UP AND DOWN AFTER SEPTEMBER 11

—Reuters headline, December 2, 2001

A Relationship on the Brinks

t's a common occurrence: Love fades; arguments erupt; couples decide to break up. It's sad and painful, but it's certainly not a newsworthy event. So when Willie Dorsey Jr. and his girlfriend, Quiana Anderson, broke up, no one should have taken notice, except for the fact that they were at work as armored car guards. Their final argument reached its pinnacle when they arrived at a bank in New Orleans and Willie jumped out of the vehicle and pointed his .357 magnum revolver at Quiana. The woman knew her relationship had shattered, but knew nothing else would shatter, since she was locked inside the vehicle's bulletproof cab. But when Willie shot off his mouth and threatened to hunt Quiana down after work and "bust a cap in her head," she waited until he went into the bank and called the police. According to an article in the *New Orleans Times-Picayune,* Willie was charged with aggravated assault after responding officers, who were very disarming, disarmed both armored car guards as an armistice and to avoid Armageddon. ♥

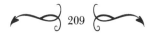

♥ ♥ ♥

In 1994, twenty-six-year-old Anna Nicole Smith, claiming she was attracted by his "kindness," married eighty-nine-year-old millionaire J. Howard Marshall.

♥ ♥ ♥

Being Accountable for Your Actions

An Albany, Indiana, woman in the middle of a divorce decided it was only fair to send her husband a bill. The bill wasn't to pay for her divorce lawyer, but for all the housework she labored over during the course of their marriage. Kathy Thompson said she kept track of her household efforts and sent her soon-to-be ex-husband, Gary, an invoice for nearly half a million dollars. The itemized statement included charges like $35,200 for cooking, $17,600 for laundry, and a paltry $1,200 for yard work. "It's not about the money. It's about standing up for women's rights and the respect they deserve and their duties around the house," proclaimed Kathy. The bill doesn't account for how much she would have charged for sex—I guess because he might have asked for a money-back guarantee. ♥

A couple having sex in the Bon Accord Terrace Gardens in Scotland had their clothes stolen, and the woman was half a mile away from home with only a newspaper to cover herself. When she arrived at her apartment she discovered that her roommate had left, the door was locked, and the keys were in her stolen jacket.

One, Two, Three, Four, Can I Have a Little More?

t must be comforting for a person to wake up after surgery to see the people who mean the most gathered around the bed. For Melvyn Reed of Kettering, Northamptonshire, England, however, it wasn't so nice when he awoke from triple bypass surgery to the faces of his three wives. While Melvyn was on the operating table getting his bypass, his life as a double bigamist suddenly reached an impasse. "Unfortunately, the timing of the visits went out of sync," he told officers when they investigated. "And they all arrived at once." When the triplets realized they all had something in common, namely Melvyn, they confronted the three-timer, and he confessed again, and again, and again. Melvyn turned himself over to the police in September 2005, was charged with bigamy, given a suspended jail term, and fined court costs of 70 pounds ($129 US). According to the *London Telegraph,* Melvyn's first wife apparently forgave him and he moved back in with her. From a triple, to a single, to a home run. ♥

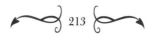

Memories Light the Corners of My Mind

Several months after meeting an unforgettable woman, Ron Scherer couldn't think of living without her; but at the same time, he couldn't think of her last name, either. All he could jostle from his memory was her first name, Kathy, and that she lived in the Dayton, Ohio, suburb of Kettering. "Now and then in your life you see an individual who strikes you a certain way. That's how I felt when I saw her," Ron said. Ron loved "Old what's-her-name" so much that he took out a $1,500 full-page ad in the *Kettering-Oakwood Times* asking "What's-her-face" to call. The ad, a modern version of the glass slipper, only generated two calls but no word from the Cinderella he sort of remembered. "If the newspaper ad doesn't work," like Ron's RAM doesn't work, "I'll try something else," he said. "Like maybe putting a sign on an airplane and flying it over Kettering." ♥

One Size Fits All

On the night before their wedding on the Greek island of Crete, a couple was celebrating with friends at separate bachelor and bachelorette parties. Friends of the bride were so excited about the next day, they couldn't wait to see her wedding gown and begged her to give them a peek. When they arrived at the house and threw open the door to surprise her fiancé, what the bride-to-be saw surprised her so much she suffered a nervous breakdown. Her friends, however, still got to see the wedding dress because the groom was wearing it. Not only was the wedding dress draped lovingly over her future husband's body, but the best man was draped lovingly over his body, too. The young bride-to-be was taken to a clinic for treatment, the wedding was canceled, and there's no word on who took possession of the wedding dress. ♥

Bride on the Side

he Runaway Bride Syndrome struck a young Romanian man named Lucien when he was jilted by his fiancée days before his wedding in Bucharest. The man's parents were crestfallen, not because their son's future wife ran away, but because they were going to lose a ton of money on the ceremony. According to the *Evenimentul Zilei* newspaper, Romanian wedding guests give money to help the parents recoup some of the expense. Without a wedding, there would be no guests; without guests, there would be no extra money; without extra money, Lucien's parents would have to pay for everything themselves. The parents figured that since the bride put a rent in their plans, they would rent a new bride. For the promise of $100, a childhood friend of Lucien's named Mariana agreed to be the stand-in bride; she rehearsed her lines for days and practiced the ceremony with the groom. The big day arrived but the big turnout didn't. Only two thirds of the expected guests attended, and some, shocked at the change of brides, weren't as generous as hoped for. Mariana, who obviously worked on a percentage basis, received only $3 instead of the $100 she was promised. Getting cheated out of money was the least of Mariana's worries—Lucien suddenly realized he loved Mariana and wanted their marriage to work. ♥

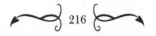

A Simple Yes or No Would Be Sufficient

A Sicilian groom who stood next to his bride-to-be and looked up into the stern face of the priest confused the guests in attendance when he answered, "I don't," to the question, "Will you take this woman to be your lawfully wedded wife." The groom's negative response wasn't a slip of the tongue, and he didn't intend to slip the ring on his fiancée's finger, either. The man planned the public denial of his love and the humiliation of his once-future bride as revenge for her unfaithfulness. The night before their wedding, the man had giddily returned from a stag party only to discover his betrothed in the arms of someone else. "It's not me you should be marrying," the groom yelled from the altar. "It's your lover, sitting in the front row, who's meant to be my witness." As expected, the wedding didn't take place. But what you might not expect is that the groom still invited all the guests to the wedding breakfast. The fiancée didn't eat with the guests, as she already had plenty of egg on her face and had eaten a big serving of crow. ♥

♥ ♥ ♥

A Malawi, Africa, court
convicted a Catholic priest and
a nun of disorderly conduct after
they were caught having sex at
Lilongwe International Airport
in a Toyota Corolla.

♥ ♥ ♥

For the Love of Lazarus

Northeast Cape Fear River has a macabre name and was the perfect place for police to look for the body of Joel Hines Jr. of Burgaw, North Carolina. The Pender County Sheriff's Department headed an exhaustive five-day search after Hines's fishing boat turned up without him in it. When Hines and his fiancée, Thelma Jones, stopped by the sheriff's office, Sergeant Philip Rivenbark decided it was safe to call off the search. Hines explained that he had been in Texas while deputies combed the surrounding areas. He said he had second thoughts about moving in with his fiancée, so he staged an accident on his fishing boat, hid in some woods, and jumped a bus to Texas. He then had third thoughts and returned to North Carolina to be reunited with Thelma. No charges were filed against Hines, but the county did ask him to repay the $5,000 spent for the search, which included, boats, dogs, and helicopters. Probably one of the most expensive games of hide-and-seek in history. ♥

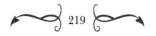

♥ ♥ ♥

In July 2002, German police responded to an elderly woman's report that frightened cries of distress had been emanating from her neighbor's yard for more than two hours. After investigating the incident, the police explained to the seventy-two-year-old witness that the noise she had heard was that of a pair of amorous hedgehogs mating.

♥ ♥ ♥

They Deserve a Break Today

Ken Sinchar pulled up to the drive-through window at a McDonald's restaurant in Pittsburgh, Pennsylvania, and requested something that wasn't on the menu—Lori Sherbondy's hand in marriage. The couple's McRomance started when they met at the drive-through, and soon their feelings for each other had Super-Sized. When it came time to pick a location for their wedding, the drive-through just seemed made to order. Lori took up her familiar position at the drive-through window and when Ken pulled up in his minivan they exchanged vows. A judge, not Mayor McCheese, performed the ceremony as the couple held hands through the window; Ken's parents sat in the backseat as witnesses (and to hold the drink tray). The September 2005 ceremony was convenient, and the service was fast. I wonder if Ken and Lori (aka Big Mac and his sexy little love McMuffin) are planning on having any small fries? ♥

One of the first pornographic films in the United States, circa 1915, was entitled *A Free Ride.* The film was created by a director identified as **A. Wise Guy** and a cinematographer named **Will B. Hard**.

—*The History of Sex,* the History Channel, August 1999

The Hindus and Don'ts of Relationships

I n New Delhi, India, a college girl who was in love with a nineteen-year-old boy decided to marry his older brother instead. Sneha Patel, a resident of the western Indian state of Gujarat, had fallen in love with Yash Kishan Parmar and wanted to marry him, but her parents opposed the marriage. The *Indian Express* reported that the legal age for marriage in India is eighteen for girls and twenty-one for boys, and shacking-up is not very popular in the tradition-steeped country. Sneha had an idea that would curry the favor of everyone; she would marry Yash's older brother, live in the same house as Yash, and then divorce the older brother when Yash reached legal marrying age. The newspaper reported that the older brother even agreed to sign a contract stating that in two years he would divorce Sneha, and that until that time he would treat her as if she were his younger brother's wife. I hate to be cynical, but I see the makings of a bad Bollywood movie here, don't you? ♥

♥ ♥ ♥

Gary Edwards of Gobowen, England, proposed to his girlfriend, Jeanette Wilson, in line at a fish and chips shop. Having thought of proposing at the spur of the moment, the man didn't have an engagement ring. But he did have an onion ring, and he slipped it on her finger. Jeanette told the *Sun:* "I hope he doesn't want to wed me in the local curry house."

♥ ♥ ♥

A Break in the Action

Yu Haitao and his bride, Fang Shuling, were in their honeymoon suite at a Shanghai hotel preparing to have a little postwedding fun and games when Yu fell off the bed and broke his arm. Fortunately, there were plenty of people to help the groom off the floor and comfort him. The room was filled with family and friends as they prepared to begin the traditional "heckle the newlyweds" game. Reuters reported in May 2005 that Yu, in anticipation of the festivities, jumped up on the bed, lost his balance, and fell. Yu and Fang then sued the hotel for negligence, stating that the bed should have been sturdier and safer to stand on. If nothing else, the couple got their marriage off to a flying start. ♥

Svetin Gulisija of Seget in Croatia was too tired to have sex with his wife, and he knew she was going to request it that night. He thought he would distract her by building a fire in the woods behind their house and then heroically rushing out to extinguish the flames. The fire quickly spread and engulfed their house, causing $23,900 in damages. The man was arrested on charges of arson and was sentenced to two years in jail.

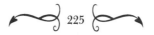

Ill-Gotten Losses

ynda Iddon, a twice-married widow, grew to hate her husband, Kenneth, and wanted him out of her life. She hated him so much, in fact, that she claimed she was disappointed when her husband beat a life-threatening form of cancer. The only thing she still liked about him was his money, and getting it was what she had her heart set on. Instead of hiring a lawyer and filing for divorce, Lynda hired several hit men who, along with her son, Lee Shergold, were ordered to kill Kenneth. On February 1, 2005, the men successfully carried out their instructions and beat and stabbed Kenneth Iddon in his driveway. Then they dragged him to the garage where they finished him off. Prosecuting attorney Peter Wright said, "Lynda Iddon had been divorced before, and she was not prepared to undergo such an experience again. She had a far swifter and more permanent way of removing Kenneth Iddon from her life, and she hoped to profit from her husband's death." Lynda, her son, and their accomplices were all arrested, but no one inherited anything except the label of murderer. Unbeknownst to Lynda, Kenneth had his will changed, leaving everything to his daughter, Gemma. ♥

An Australian doctor diagnosed one of his patients as having a rare sleeping disorder that caused her to have sex with strangers while she slumbered.

♥ ♥ ♥

Ronald Krischbaum was charged with misdemeanor exposure, lewdness, and resisting arrest after Delaware state police found him dancing on the shoulder of I-95 wearing nothing but a woman's bra and panties on his head.

FOR VALENTINE'S DAY, TRY TO PLAN YOUR SPONTANEITY

—Indianapolis Star, February 12, 2003

Broadcast News

Radio advice host Paula White took the advice of her listeners when she confessed on air that her husband was having an affair with a secretary at her office. In an interview with the *Mirror,* Paula, of *Paula White's Phone In,* said, "I found a text message on my husband's phone which was very personal and very private and I shouldn't have read it. And it was signed Andy. My immediate reaction was, 'Oh my God, he's gay.' I confronted him. He told me I was paranoid, and it wasn't true, and stormed off. Then he came downstairs and told me he was having an affair, but it was with another woman. It was the first time I had suspected anything." The program, heard on Century FM, generated two hundred calls of support for Paula, most offering her advice on how to handle the situation. "People were telling me how they coped with the same situation. One woman said, 'Don't call him a dog because dogs are faithful, and it's unfair to them,'" the "Agony Aunt" said. "There were people who I had given advice to who were ringing back to leave messages of support. It was the busiest night we had ever had—two hundred calls. But not one person said I should take him back." Apparently Paula and her husband had either radio silence or some serious static at home that Paula had chosen to tune out. ♥

♥ ♥ ♥

Homosexual acts remain punishable by death in Afghanistan, Mauritania, Iran, Nigeria, Pakistan, Saudi Arabia, Sudan, United Arab Emirates, and Yemen, and by life in prison in Bangladesh, Bhutan, Guyana, India, Maldives, Nepal, Singapore, and Uganda.

♥ ♥ ♥

Fat Chance

A Romanian woman told a divorce court in Focsani that she wanted to leave her husband because she was envious of his metabolism. Maria Alexandru complained to the court that her husband, Toader, never gained weight regardless of what he ate. She said she couldn't bear watching him stuff himself and never gain a pound when she only had to look at food to put on weight. So I guess she thought the best way to loose a few hundred pounds was to get rid of her husband. ♥

A German man drove his car into a road sign at sixty mph and was eventually charged 600 euros for leaving the scene of a hit-and-run accident. When the man was apprehended, he said the cause of the accident was that his **visibility** had been blocked: He was making love to a blonde **hitchhiker** when he lost control of the vehicle.

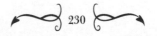

Drinks Are on the House

Barmaid Hilary Hammans was fired for flirting with one of her customers and sued her employer to get her job back. What makes this case unique is that Hilary's boss was also her husband and the couple lived where they worked, the Fox Inn in Steventon, Oxfordshire. Hilary's flirtations with a golfer were determined to be serious when Larry Hammans cross-examined her at trial. He asked how she "managed to buy a £1,000 set of golf clubs when her bank statement showed she only paid £100." Hilary was close to tears as she told the divorce tribunal: "My life has been turned upside down. There was no breakdown in our working relationship." But bar owner and landlord Larry saw things differently: "I still want my wife back; we still live in the house. But you can only work together in a pub as man and wife. . . . There has got to be that magnetism and respect for each other. You say our relationship was good behind the bar, but we weren't even talking." The tribunal ruled that Hilary had been unfairly dismissed, and the couple shared some parting words: "I got what I came for," said Hilary. "I'll see you at home," said Larry. ♥

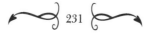

♥ ♥ ♥

A member of the British House of Lords, Norman Tebbit, told a radio interviewer that homosexuality in Britain is "intimately connected" to the rise in obesity. He explained that homosexuality was causing a breakdown of the traditional family and that meant fewer family meals and more fattening fast food.

♥ ♥ ♥

A Pack of Trouble

nternationally famous blonde bombshell (okay, former blonde bombshell) Brigitte Bardot appeared on Romanian television pleading with citizens to adopt stray dogs before the animals are put down. Mariana Ghiorghiu was so moved by the film star's call to action that she went out and fetched five four-legged friends and brought them home. When her husband, George, arrived from work and discovered the five new pets, he unleashed this threat, "It's either me or the dogs!" To his surprise, Mariana told him she would rather have a shih tzu, and suggested he take himself for a walk or just hop the next Greyhound out of town. Instead of rolling up a newspaper and hitting George on the nose, she filed for divorce the next day. ♥

In response to reports of Chinese **espionage**, Department of Energy security guidelines were modified in August 1999 to include a requirement that workers report any "close and continuing contact" (defined as two or more visits) with nationals from twenty-five specified countries. DOE official Edward Curran explained to reporters that ongoing sexual relationships are covered but that **one-night stands** are not. He defended the new requirements saying they would neither undermine romance or encourage **promiscuity**.

Highways and Bye-Ways

on't drink and drive" is a slogan we've all heard and hopefully observed, but a phrase that speaks to an even greater danger is "Don't drink and drive and argue with your wife." After several drinks at a pub in Middleton, England, Terry Mangan and his wife, Joanne, were on their way home in Liverpool when an argument broke out. The argument began when Joanne accused her husband of flirting with a barmaid, and it ended when Terry struck her, stopped on the M62 motorway, and got out of the car. Joanne slipped into the driver's seat and pulled back onto the highway when Terry jumped onto the hood of the vehicle. In order "to teach him a lesson about how dangerous it was to stop on the motorway," Joanne said, she stepped on the gas. It was a lesson well learned. Terry fell off the hood of the car and into the path of a truck that ran him over and killed him. Joanne was charged with manslaughter and DUI, but the Crown Prosecution Service later dropped the charges. ♥

Ms. Christelle Demichel wed her sweetheart, Eric, at a ceremony in Nice, France, in February 2004. The groom was stiff as a board, not because he was scared, but because he was dead. The man had been killed by a drunk driver in 2002, but French law allowed the marriage to proceed, as the paperwork had been completed and President Chirac had approved their union.

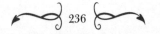

A Nonperishable Memory

t's a brilliant ice breaker," said Ian Roberson of Treharris, England. "Now when I meet women I just ask the girls if they want to see my plums and roll up my sleeve." What he reveals when he rolls up his sleeve is a tattoo. But it's not an eagle, or the word "Mom," or a heart with an arrow through it—it's a can of tomatoes. When Ian's wife, Susan, walked out after ten years of marriage, she not only left him brokenhearted, but also left him with only a can of Prince's plum tomatoes in the kitchen. The story of the tin of tomatoes brought a lot of canned laughter to Ian's friends at the pub, so he decided to stop stewing and have some fun. "Now every time I look at the tattoo, it reminds me of the day my wife walked out," Ian said. But the can of tomatoes on his arm wasn't put there just to symbolize the tomato that walked out of his life—Ian also had it done on the condition his pub friends help him raise 500 pounds for a villager suffering from a rare form of cancer. I'm sure other people have noticed that the name Prince doesn't just refer to the name on the tomato can. ♥

Abstinence advocate Pat Socia told a crowd of teenagers
at a high school sex-education rally in Chicago in April 2000
that if they felt a sexual urge coming on,
"Just eat a **Snickers** bar. You'll be fine!"

In January 2000, Quebec researcher Jim Pfaus drew a
comparison between rats and human males, the *Montreal Gazette*
reported. Pfaus's studies showed that rats are always
on the lookout to copulate with new females, and if those rats
are given **alcohol**, they will reattempt to have sex
with a female who has just **rejected** them.

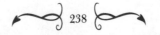

A Shrink in Time ...

A Canadian couple was seeing a marriage counselor, but things kept getting worse instead of better, and they finally divorced. It was sometime after their divorce that the man finally found out what had gone wrong in their marriage—his wife was sleeping with their marriage counselor. Apparently, the psychologist had been using his couch to delve into more than the woman's private thoughts. The Alberta Court of Queen's Bench gave the psychologist a Freudian pink slip and charged him with breach of duty. Since the trial, the woman has been stricken with a debilitating, chronic disease, and she has moved back in with her estranged husband so he can help care for her. Love conquers all. ♥

Sparring and Paring

A husband's dereliction of domestic duties is a source of conflict for a lot of couples. Anjalee Allen asked her husband, David, if he could clean up the lunch dishes, and he said he would. David couched the idea of KP and jumped on the couch for some R&R. When he woke up, he and Anjalee got into a huge fight. Anjalee grabbed a dirty vegetable knife and stuck it clean into David's heart. According to *News of the World,* David was rushed to the hospital for emergency open-heart surgery. David recalled, "She was livid and grabbed the knife. The next thing she seemed to slap at me and the blade hit my chest. It was just bad luck that the knife went so deep." Although David didn't press charges, the Crown Prosecution Service decided to go ahead with the case after Anjalee pleaded guilty. Getting stabbed in the chest gave David a new handle on their relationship: "I have now made a full recovery and have forgiven my wife. If anything, this has brought us closer." If this is true, then David is obviously not the sharpest knife in the drawer. ♥

♥ ♥ ♥

Senator Felix Salgado of the Mexican legislature spoke out against adopting daylight saving time, as it would curb many *mananeros'*, or couples', morning lovemaking. "[N]ow when you wake up," said Salgado in March 2000, "your partner is no longer there because she had to take the kids to school."

♥ ♥ ♥

Boys in the 'Hood

After ten years of marriage, an English couple divorced. The husband moved out, and the man with whom the wife was having an affair moved in. The former husband got a nice little council home (public housing) in Hartlepool and began his life anew by decorating his house. "There goes the neighborhood" had to be running through the man's mind when he looked out the window to see a familiar man moving into the house next door. It was his wife's lover. She had kicked him out of the house, and he was forced to find an inexpensive place to live. The man complained to authorities saying that it would be unbearable living next to his replacement. Local government ombudsman Patricia Smith ruled that the man should not be given the house, but not because of his past relationship with the other man's former wife. Turns out he didn't qualify under the current council points system. Hartlepool Borough Council agreed to pay the aggrieved former tenant 1,600 pounds to cover the expenses he incurred decorating his house and for the trouble the incident caused him. ♥

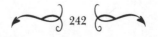

Film at Eleven

A Romanian man who hadn't seen his ex-wife in two years suffered a fatal heart attack when he first saw her again. Sandu Cojanis invited some friends over to his house, and one of them brought a pornographic film. According to the local daily, the friend popped the video into the VCR, hit play, and Sandu hit the floor—his ex-wife was one of the coming attractions. It was not reported how the friends took care of Sandu's body after the heart attack or even if they stayed and finished watching the movie. ♥

CALL FOR SUBMISSIONS: SEX WORKER ANTHOLOGY

—Company Press Release, September 4, 2005

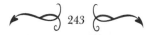

♥ ♥ ♥

"I tried to follow the ways of Jesus, to get back to the basics of Christianity," said former United Church minister Anthony Gifford before his sexual assault trial. Gifford admitted having had consensual sex with troubled female parishioners but said he was only counseling them.

♥ ♥ ♥

A Sign of the Times

A wife from Worcester, England, said there were too many signs that her husband's obsession was getting in the way of their marriage. Graham Stanton spent over twenty-five years collecting road signs that filled several rooms in their house. His fascination began after he looked in a hedge and found a sign reading MEN AT WORK (a warning, not the eighties Australian rock band). His seven-hundred-plus-piece collection included a two-hundred-year-old milestone and NO U-TURN signs, the *Sun* reported. Lynne sent him a warning sign: If you don't store those signs in a warehouse instead of our house, one collector's item you'll be missing is me!"

"People think I'm barking [crazy], but my collection is unique," said Graham (so unique, in fact, that collectors in Bilbao, Spain, have named a street, Avenida Graham Stanton, in his honor). "Lynne didn't seem to mind when it filled the garage, but then it spread to the house. I hoped she'd see the HALT signs as unusual ornaments, but they got on her nerves. Now I'll have to keep them somewhere that doesn't drive her mad." I'm sure the couple will reach some sort of collective agreement soon. ♥

In support of the government's campaign to raise the birth rate, Singapore's leading newspaper published a **how-to** guide to making love in cars.

In September 1999, Italy's Court of Cassation ruled that a woman had broken her marriage vows even though she never had a personal or sexual relationship with another man. However, the court ruled, the woman's **constant** thoughts about a local bus driver had broken the "trust and intimacy" of her marriage just as surely as if the two had had sex.

In Need of a Head Cleaner

woman in Fargo, North Dakota, went to a judge to get a restraining order against her ex-boyfriend, Justin Fraase. Justin must have thought the restraining order made him out to be a bad guy, and he came up with a way to prove to the police that his former girlfriend wasn't really afraid of him. He reasoned that if he showed the police a videotape of the two of them making love, they would realize the restraining order was a mistake and revoke it. He presented such a videotape to the Fargo police and waited smugly for them to see things his way. After screening the video, officers immediately contacted the unnamed woman to get her side of the story. She told the officers Justin had persuaded her to come to his apartment under the pretext of discussing the custody of their two children, and once inside he attacked and raped her. The video was the evidence needed to charge Justin with gross sexual imposition, assault, felonious restraint, and violation of a protection order. Investigators said the woman could be heard on the video protesting and struggling against his unwanted advances. "He obviously didn't watch it before he gave it to us," a police investigator said. ♥

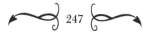

♥ ♥ ♥

In third-century India, men sometimes taught their parrots dirty words and phrases to help them seduce women.

—*The History of Sex*, the History Channel, August 1999

The Numbers Don't Lie

Charles Edward Hicks of Fairfax County, Virginia, has been a very busy man, and either he is very forgetful or he enjoys living under extreme pressure. Charles has been married seven times over the past forty years and has had a hard time letting go of some of his wives—so he has just stayed married to them. Assistant Commonwealth's Attorney Katie Swart has charged Charles with bigamy but, oh, if it were only that simple. You see, when Charles married wife number seven he was still married to wife number six. But the legality of his marriage to number six is in question because he might have still been married to wife number five. He was granted a divorce from number five three weeks after being charged on bigamy for number seven and number six. Now, number six has asked prosecutors to charge him with bigamy for the marriages of number six and number five. Attorney Swart has dropped all charges against Charles until she can sort things out—and get rid of her migraine. ♥

♥ ♥ ♥

A postal worker from Edinburgh, Scotland, Graham Fletcher, was sentenced to community service for failure to deliver 2 items (reduced from the original 696 items). Fletcher said he began hoarding mail after he fell into a depression caused by seeing his wife kissing another man outside a bar during a ladies'-night-out celebration.

♥ ♥ ♥

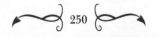

It's My Party and I'll &%!# If I Want To

Swedish police busted a group sex party at a Molndal hotel between a Norwegian woman, her husband, and seven other naked men. Authorities reported the host and hostess advertised their Tupperware party online and drew nearly five hundred responses, which they pared down to fifteen invited guests who paid $45 apiece for a piece. Police watched the activities for thirty minutes and then arrested two participants on charges of buying sex, which *Espressen,* the Swedish newspaper, reported is the first case of its kind in Swedish history. The irony of this situation is had the couple had their little party in their home country of Norway, nothing would have happened—in Norway it isn't illegal to purchase sex. ♥

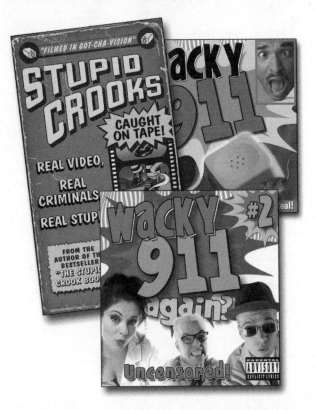